THE GIFT of GOD

CHANGING YOUR HEART AND MIND TO RECEIVE AND NOT BE DECEIVED

PROPHETESS GRACE LOPEZ

WESTBOW
PRESS®
A DIVISION OF THOMAS NELSON
& ZONDERVAN

WestBow Press books may be ordered through booksellers or by contacting:

WestBow Press
A Division of Thomas Nelson & Zondervan
1663 Liberty Drive
Bloomington, IN 47403
www.westbowpress.com
844-714-3454

All Scripture quotations are taken from the Holy Bible, NEW INTERNATIONAL VERSION®, NIV® Copyright © 1973, 1978, 1984, 2011 by Biblica, Inc.® Used by permission. All rights reserved worldwide.

ISBN: 979-8-3850-0236-8 (sc)
ISBN: 979-8-3850-0237-5 (e)

Library of Congress Control Number: 2023913089

Print information available on the last page.

WestBow Press rev. date: 08/17/2023

I thank you Lord,
that you have a destiny for me.

You have set before me plans to prosper me
in all areas of my life.

Your Word makes possible for me
to recognize the true gift
that you purchased
and freely gave me.

Thank you, Jesus,
for creating in me the anointing of
purposeful living and prophesy.

May this message bring God the glory
and bless those who receive themselves,
His revelation, His gift.

Dedication

I remember my mother would set time aside to sit and pray, daily. As I would sit at her feet, I can recall how she prayed. She would begin by talking to God, it wasn't any kind of recited prayer other than the Lord's prayer.

She would talk to him about her problems, thank Him for the successes, and request a covering for her children, her family, and other people. She always was at peace while praying and even looked relieved. It is through seeing her, listening to her pray, and seeing how great her faith was, that I followed her method of prayer. There were many things that my mother taught me, the most valuable was having a relationship with God. My mom was my role model, a good parent, a great teacher, a strong woman, and a faithful believer in God.

Acknowledgment

To my children and GRANDchildren
Cassandra, Carlos III, Candice
Westyn, and Damani

The divine purpose that Jesus,
my Lord,
set in place through vision and prophesy,
was the creation of this book
as a spiritual inheritance for you.

I thank Jesus that His inspired Word became my reality.
I pray that His Word will stir in you
the determination to find yours.

Susie J Carreon [Avelar]:
You have been my stability, my heart, the friend
who is greater than a sister,
and my voice of reason.
You have honored God and continue to be
an inspiration to many lives.
Your demonstration of commitment
preserves who you are and is a reflection
of the love God intended for each of us.
You are truly a Gift of God.

**Anointed Body of Jesus Ministry,
Rev. Dale Rhames:**
Thank you for your support thru prayer and encouragement.
Your passion and knowledge for the Word of God
has been inspiring and instrumental
in the making of this message.

Joe & Leslie [Heiden] Simental
Thank you that you followed the instruction
of the Lord and were the warriors who
introduced me, on that Sunday at Desert Chapel,
to hear the Word of God.
I accepted Jesus which changed
the direction of my life forever.
I have loved you and your children and
will continue to, always.

Honorable Mention:
And to those who have been so influential
in my life [past and present], I thank the Lord that He allowed
you to enable me to receive His wisdom and revelation from
my presence in relationship. The time spent with you was and
is all a part of the plan for my deeper understanding of the
greatest gift my Heavenly Father has given me. Thank you.

His Word is my living
and abiding constant voice.
Amen

To better understand who and what we are we must first start at the beginning.

The Word of God clearly says, *In the beginning, God.*

These aren't just the first four [4] words of the bible. These words are the inception and outline for our life. These first four words are the summary of the whole story of the Bible, the story of God.

God always makes the first [and last] move in everything. He was there in the beginning and will be here in the end.

There are several things that these first four words do.

- ❖ God saw, He thought, He spoke and immediately "acted".
- ❖ His first intention was for you and me.
- ❖ God reached out to man, He sought us – first.
- ❖ His character is one of initiative, He created the heavens and the earth and all its contents for you and I.
- ❖ God took the initiative to communicate to us His nature and His will from the very beginning.
- ❖ God used the Prophets in the past, to speak to His people.
- ❖ God today speaks to us by His Son [1] and thru the Holy Spirit.

He thought of all this, **in the beginning**.

God created, God spoke, and through Jesus He operated, for our benefit.

God is immortal and infinite. We are mortal and finite. Our minds, without Jesus, cannot understand the things of God. We would be

---

[1] Heb.1:1,2 God who at various times and in various ways spoke in time past to the fathers by the prophets, has in these last days spoken to us by His Son…

in a crisis if we didn't have a remedy for this state. But God, ah yes, but God. He once acted, in the beginning, and again He acts for us on our behalf.

Our remedy for this situation is Jesus.

This is the Gospel, the Truth.

God spoke and He revealed himself. His actions, nonetheless, selfless, were the foundation for us. He has laid out the formula, the foundation of His relationship with us. We must follow His design. He first saw, thought, and then spoke or acted. This is the formula for us. We must first see [what God has provided and/or allowed], then think as God would [through the Holy Spirit], and finally act upon as God would [us seeking the Lord in every decision].

We have all been taught, or have read part of His revelation, His nature, His will – but only in part. To fully understand him we must be accepting of his greatest gift…Jesus.

God in His magnificent wisdom knew that he would need to set up the facts for proof of the majesty and miraculous human of all; the birth of the perfect man in flesh – Jesus.

It is through our personal relationship with Jesus that we receive knowledge of His existence, His divine power, His glory, His faithfulness, and His love for us.

Through Jesus, the gift of God to us, we can find the deep things of God[2]. Without accepting Jesus, we deny the Gift of God and miss knowing who we are and what he has planned for us.

---

[2] Job 11:7 "Can you search out the deep things of God? Can you find out the limits of the Almighty?

God in his vast thoughts [in the beginning] and his love toward us, enabled us to know him thru His Word[3] Even in this day and age, there is no other faith/religion that can compare with the message of God – who loved, came after us, and died for a world of lost sinners to provide for us an eternal life. He created the way where there was none. Without the resurrection of Jesus, God's gift to us, we had no eternal life.

There was no one able to give us the salvation needed to enter the

Kingdom of God.

This statement involves the rethinking of our whole outlook.

Rethinking life, reconsidering the position of God – our creator.

In seeking the knowledge and understanding of whom I am, required the understanding of whom I came from. You can only find the answer through His Word. The Word of life, the Word of truth.

Many have opted to seek wisdom from the world, as society dictates and defines who we are. If you are defined by a society and not by God, then you are misled and misinformed – you are being lied to.

God's Word is truth and life – why would you seek an answer from anyone other than your creator who knows you better than anyone could ever attempt to know you.

Society has continually told us who they believe we are and what is expected of us. What the world is not telling you is

the truth.

---

[3] JohTn 1:1, 14 In the beginning was the Word, and the Word was with God, and the Word was God. And the Word became flesh and dwelt among us...

Their definition does not line up and cannot line up unless is it established from God's Word. The world attempts to tell us "truth" but melds their version[s] and way of thinking. This cannot be truth because it is founded on man's way of thinking and living, not established on God's way of thinking, and living.

We live in a world that is not based on God's Word but a facade of it. The world will manipulate the truth to lead our way of thinking into a direction that is comfortable for us. We were put in this world not to be unhappy or not to be able to enjoy the good things of life, right? This is what the world tells you. The Word of God tells us that we were created...created in His image. We did not evolve, and we were not put here. God created us and breathed His breath of life into us- In the beginning.

To know who you are, you must know where you came from. Amen.

In the beginning, at the time of creation, was the Word. The eternal logos – the Word. The Word was with God, giving us the example of the beginning of relationship. The Word was *with* God. God was in the beginning and is now. God, our creator, He created you. God created for 5 days and saw His splendor and knew it was good. He stated so. God is a God of order; He set up everything so that man would be blessed by His created world for him to enjoy and use of it. He created such a beauty and all that we could ever want or need and decided it was time for you and me to come into existence – on the 6th day He created you.

You are His conception, made into existence. When He created you, in His own image, He created the image of righteousness, matchlessness and all holiness. He created us to be different than the animals and the vegetation. We were created upright, created to be more splendid than His creation of all the earth. God took his time to create the heavens and the earth to make it good but made us more marvelous and to enjoy it all. This was His will for us. His creation of the earth and all therein was made for our enjoyment. Every good and perfect gift comes from above[4]. God, the creator of all good and perfect gifts. When He created the earth and gave us dominion over all the earth, he "gave" us the example to follow - His gift, the gift of His completed creation. He then reflected on the 7th day and was pleased.

After he created man, he knew that man needed a helpmate and created Eve from the rib of Adam. He was aware that man could not live alone and wanted Adam to perceive the gift of a mate [one that would help and support], to understand the meaningful gift through marriage, and to live a life with connection – family.

The greater gift He gave us was telling us that we are:

Blessed
> God's creation of the earth and all that is in it was perfectly made just for you to enjoy it. He spoke His blessing over us.

A ruler
> God gave you dominion over all the earth. Command over all living things. To be as Kingly heirs.

Highly recognized
> God set you over all things, to rule and be set apart. He created you to be higher than the animals,

---

[4] James 1:17 Every good gift and every perfect gift is from above, and comes down from the Father of lights, with whom there is no variation or shadow of turning.

trees, fowl, and every beast of the field[5]. We must acknowledge our position He placed on us.

Righteous and perfectly made
You were made in His image – God's likeness[6].

God-breathed
Not only did he create you, but he also breathed His breath of life into you. You were given life through his breath[7]

Complete
After God saw all that he formed, He was incredibly pleased and was at peace. Because you are complete in all through Him, you can be at peace. You need to know that there is nothing missing, nothing wrong, and you are fashioned perfectly because you were made by the Creator.

Perfection – God.
You are his finished product.

---

[5] Gen 1:28-30 Then God blessed them, and God said to them, "Be fruitful and multiply: fill the earth and subdue it: have dominion over the fish of the sea, over the birds of the air, and over every living thing that moves on the earth." And God said, "See, I have given you every herb that yields seed which is on the face of all the earth, and every tree whose fruit yields seed: to you it shall be for food. "Also, to every beast of the earth, to every bird of the air, and to everything that creeps on the earth, in which there is life, I have given every green herb for food; and it was so.

[6] Gen 1:27 So God created man in His own image; in the image of God, He created him; male and female He created them.

[7] Gen 2:7 And the Lord God formed man of the dust of the ground and breathed into his nostrils the breath of life; and man became a living being.

Because of the disobedience of Adam, we altered the state of completion that was intended by our Father. By eating of the Tree of Good and Evil, Adam & Eve now understood and knew evil. Their eyes were opened to understand evil. Before their disobedience what they knew was only good[8]. This is the character of God, our Father. His desire to keep His creation safe, taken care of, having no want or need that was not already foreseen and to have their minds and heart filled with goodness and love towards Him. This is the heart of God. This is His demonstration to us of his generosity, his desire, his plan, but more importantly – his love towards us. Unfortunately, man blew it! Eve chose to believe something that had no connection to her, a thought that was derived with the intent only to gift her with the opposite of God's intent. Adam forgot what Eve's role was in relation to him. She was created to be his helper, to aid him, and to support him. Once Eve obeyed the serpent, she diminished her position of aid to Adam.

She took upon herself a position of headship. She did not confer with Adam, she decided for herself not considering how that would directly impact both, not just herself. As Adam's helper, she was created to complete him so that the process of being fruitful and multiply would be accomplished. God could have very easily created more than one Adam and Eve. Why he did not is something that we can only have a variety of opinions about. The fact that he created Eve to be Adam's helper, his mate, his support or rather, aid and companion is another testament of his love for his creation.

---

[8] Gen 1:28-30 Then God blessed them and God said to them, "Be fruitful and multiply; fill the earth and subdue it; have dominion over the fish of the sea, over the birds of the air, and over every living thing that moves on the earth." And God said, "See, I have given you every herb that yields seed which is on the face of all the earth, to every bird of the air, and to everything that creeps on the earth, in which there is life, I have given every green herb for food; and it was so.

We know that when God created man, it was his finished product, in part. His created being was finished but not in the spiritual aspect. We are not completed yet. We are a work in progress. The more we continue to allow the Lord to change us, the more we become closer to the original created being he intended us to be. His original intent was to be at one with Adam and Eve, with you and me. To have that relation with His children. We know how important it is that Father's have a relationship, a connection to their children. It is through the connection and communication that fathers can feel at one with their offspring. Their connection enables them to empathize, impart, and enrich their child's life. God's concern that Adam and Eve's focus were set on good and not the things of evil. This is what we want for our children as well. You see "in the beginning God" continues to set the example and if we pay close attention, we can see his loving nature behind everything that He did and continues to do for us.

Understanding what God's character and nature is, we can begin to understand who we are and can continue to allow God to work on his creation – you.

Let us examine a few things that will help us understand who we are.

The Word of God continues to tell us who we are and what we are. God began His story as a King, a ruler. He created us in His image – to rule and enjoy the creation of the gifted land as one would enjoy the benefits of his kingdom.

What is the difference between who and what we are?

Who we are is a declaration that requires knowledge of where we came from. It goes beyond who my parents are or who my people [descendants] are. God created you.

If you can agree that God first created you, then God made you perfect. No more complaining about all our perceived deficiencies or imperfections that the world says you are or possess. God made you and God does not and cannot make mistakes nor create imperfections. He created you just as you are – His finished product – perfect – in the beginning before the fall of man.

Before Adam sinned. He took his time, he thought of everything. He thought of the inside of your body, every vein, vessel, nerve, ligament, space, bone, organ, and function of it. He went beyond the physical and placed a brain that can think, react, hope, and see beyond the physical eye and see the spiritual in multi dimensions. He formed our bodies with the ability to feel, see, speak, taste, and hear, to have inner sensations and strength from a place not always understood. He was meticulous in His thought for the physical to co-exist with the internal, the spiritual. It is when we have the mind of Christ[9] that we have the understanding of His will for us. We must think with a divine intellect in thought, feeling or will of God and this is accomplished when we allow God, through the Holy Spirit to be our helper. How great is the love of God regarding us.

It is amazing to receive the concept that we have perfect love flowing through us and lack nothing. God, our Creator, considered everything about you. When He created you and me, He made us out of love because that is who He is. He considered us not in the physical manner but rather in the spiritual. Perfect Love. If we have God's love in us, through Jesus, there should be absolutely no reason that we cannot love ourselves.

Many women have shared with me how hard it is to love themselves.

---

[9] 1 Cor 2:16 For who has known the mind of Christ, that he may instruct him? But we have the mind of Christ.

I used to ponder the thought and then realize that without the knowledge of God's greatest gift - the gift of love [Christ]; it is difficult to love yourself. Comments like, "I can't love myself", are often spoken because they do not know who they are. God's love for us is so great and a testament for us through Jesus. "For God so loved the world that He gave his only begotten son..." John 3:16. God freely gave His son, who is love, to us. When we obtain [receive] this gift, we accept God's love in its entirety. God does not give gifts in part [batteries not included type of gift]; he gives us gifts in entirety. We have the sum of His love. Knowing this, accepting this truth, we must and should love ourselves. This is who you are. Because you have accepted Christ in your heart, you have His love. You are a child who is love, is derived from love, and can also love.

It is when we do not accept or believe this, that we begin to believe the lies that society has laid out for anyone who chooses to accept them. Believing the enemy, the father of all lies – Satan becomes your truth.

It is easy to settle it in your mind because there are so many supporters out there willing to tell you who they think you are rather than telling you what God says.

We begin to accept as truth a lie that perpetuates into more lies with more intensity. Even though their inner man is telling you via a hurting heart, headaches, and sadness they consent to the lie. The evidence begins manifesting as we allow ourselves to be subject to ridicule, rudeness, disrespect, hurt and pain.

As time goes on, and there is no renewing of the mind, this lie becomes a state of mind for the brokenhearted. Many end up settling for a life that is far from the plans and hopes that Christ has laid out for them. This was the intent that the serpent had for Eve. Her eyes were open to good, but Satan's intent was to open her eyes to evil. This is the evil that your eyes are opened to. Far from good and divine.

Scripture tells us exactly what the Lord's plans are for you and me[10]. They are good plans. None of the plans he has for you are like those set by society because society tells you that you must be validated by someone or something.

The Word of God tells us that you were made in His image. He has placed in you, traits that are unmatched and first rate. His plans are not temporal, but eternal. It is the plans that provide hope and an eternal future. You are full of hope, goodness, and knowledge[11].

The world will tell you the importance of relationships but has no real understanding and defines it with a rating system that is based on the physical – the chemistry between each other.

When God created Eve for Adam, he created her to be his helpmate. To be Adam's support and companion. God knew he needed her. She needed his rib to become one flesh – *Ishshah* Woman. God thought of relationship from the beginning. Forming Eve from Adam was to provide relationship with each other and together having relationship with God; together as one with him. Relationship is a God-ordained truth. He built that need in us, otherwise Adam could have been content with all that God had created in the earth.

God knew how important connection, communication and completeness was for his creation, and so he provided Eve.

---

[10] Jer 29:11 For I know the plans I have for you; declares the Lord, plans to prosper you and not to harm you, plans to give you a hope and a future.
[11] Rom 15:13 Now may the God of hope fill you with all joy and peace in believing that you may abound in hope by the power of the Holy Spirit.

Relationships are not about validation; recognizing that persons are worthwhile. Validation was given, "in the beginning" when he fashioned Adam and then Eve.

God enjoyed his creation, was pleased, and loved spending time with both of them. He gave them everything. There was nothing that they could ever want or need that God had not already made provision for. This is his character to be our Jehovah Jireh, the God of all provision for us. How much love was demonstrated to them, to have the whole earth and all that is within it and be the sole owners of it. God gifted them the world. No lack, no need for anything.

As you have and/or will come to understand, and receive his gift we too are in that same place that Adam and Eve were in. He created, in the beginning, for us all that we could ever want or need in abundance. The King of Kings has not changed. Jesus is the same today. We have the same ability to receive all that God has for us – a gift that is freely given. That is the affirmation that we need to believe in. He values us so much that all that is, is available to us, He has already provided it for us to take. God considered all that He made and when all of it was good, he made us to be able to enjoy it all with him.

He completed ALL that he made for us. Trees with ripe fruit, a garden with herbs already grown, and vegetables ready for picking. Adam and Eve did not have to wait for a fruit tree to mature to provide them the fruit. It was already made available, mature tree producing fruit. Vegetables already ripe and ready for nourishment to their body. There was no stipulations to His giving,

His provisions.

That is a testament of His love for us. He made good and perfect gifts for you and me to enjoy. There was no labor required for Adam.

God and Adam walked together, in the garden, to enjoy the splendor of it all. A gift to him to enjoy.

All these gifts come from Him, and the recipient endpoint is you. As previously stated, God makes the first and last move, with us in mind.

Because God values you and is about relationship with you, He will not fail or forsake you.

When you place your trust in man, a worldly man, failure is inevitable. Why? A worldly man is just that a man/woman who sets their foundational beliefs on what the world considers truth. When their origin is a truth described by the world and not from God, truth becomes a misrepresentation, and many are misled and derailed from the path laid out by God.

Remember God has told us that He knows the plans He has for us. Because he loves us so much, we must have confidence in that truth and accept His plans[12]. If we believe this, then we must put value behind this truth and therefore put value in ourselves. God wants the best for us, nothing less. What God has planned for us cannot be anything less than anything good.

God is a great God, not a lesser god. He cannot be anything but great – He is God. He is the King of all Kings. Because he is God, he has given you a talent that is superior – no man will give it all to you like God has. Man will always withhold something because of their selfishness and inability to desire more for you. God desires all that is good for you and me. There are few people that can say that. They cannot and will not desire all that is good for you and then provide it to you unselfishly. They will undoubtedly withhold something.

---

[12] Jer 29:11 For I know the thoughts that I think toward you, says the Lord, thoughts of peace and not of evil, to give you a future and a hope.

The relationship that God wants to have with you is unselfish and giving. He wants to give you all his gifts, freely, and only desires that you be in relationship with him. To believe in him, to receive his gifts, to put him in the proper position in your life – first position. A place of importance, a place duly deserved and most importantly a place derived from love towards him. Acknowledging that He is your King that He rules over you, over your life is the position we must take. He is your Superior, your authority. This is a foundational principle. If you are associated with a faith-based church, this must be their foundational conviction. Christ is your authority and ruler over you. He is your Father, your Creator and your God.

As a parent who loves their child, we will always take into consideration, our children first. God provided this example; in the beginning He considered us. God loves you so much that He calls you His beloved[13].

The Word of God [Bible] gives us many truths about who our creator says you are. These insights are meant for us to create new awareness so that you are no longer misled and miss out of all the benefits of God's truth. Putting on the mind of Christ. Receiving His truths is your reward, the receipt of His gift to you.

Meditate in His truth until it becomes your way of thinking, your way of life.

This is who you are:

- God says that you are fully able.
- You have God-given ability.
- He has given you sanctifying peace. A serenity that has finality, you are serene unlike no other type of tranquility.

---

[13] Col 3:12 Therefore, as the elect of God, holy and beloved...

- You are prosperous…in everything. God considers all your needs and gives you the ultimate level of provision.
- You are blessed, receiving benefits daily. Not occasionally, but each day as you purpose to receive. Planning to receive.
- His blessings are never-ending unless you choose not to receive them.
- You are full of hope, goodness, and knowledge. He has placed in you, traits that are unmatched and first rate. Making that decision to eat of the tree of life only.
- You are life-giving. Made to reproduce and continue the good of Him with our lives. Being that parent who sets the examples as Christ did.
- You are an ambassador, the highest appointment. He chose that you become His representative, a reflection of Him. Ensuring that all you say and do is based on His principles and not ours or those of the world.
- You are motivated and honest…to the Christian lifestyle. Because God has given you the answer, you are motivated to represent God in such a manner that is honorable.
- You are forgiven. No matter your past – He chooses to "forget" your past and make you aware that there is only one way He sees you – sinless, righteous and partakers of eternal life through Him, our Savior. Forgive and forget. Unlike most say, I will forgive but not forget. This is contrary to God's teaching. He forgave and never remembers your sin again[14].
- You are justified, redeemed, and have access to Him. He has given you the "free pass" card that gives you full entrance to His heavenly realm as well as you are enabled to access all His benefits freely.

---

[14] Psalm 103:12 As far as the east is from the west, so far has he removed our transgressions from us…

- You are more than conquerors. He has placed a spirit of boldness within you.
- He has given you victory over your bodies with the knowledge that your battles have already been won. He is your Jehovah-Nissi.
- You are victorious and have dominion. He does not allow fear to come near you but teaches you that you are more than able to accomplish and have power over situations. This is the attitude that David had over Goliath. David knew that Goliath came with a sword and spear. David came at Goliath with the Lord Almighty, the God of the armies of Israel[15].
- You are God's gift. Intact, complete. Given from the highest honor to be appreciated and valued by others. Favor followes you.
- You are anointed with gladness. Happiness, joy, and delight are flowing and covering you.
- You are endowed with boldness. Courage, bravery, and valor have been gifted to you.
- You are His, He chose you, the bride of Christ. Holding you up to a higher standard because of the deeper and committed relationship that we have thru Him.
- You are God's loved ones, His beloved.
- You are a righteous people, clothed with faithfulness, comforted, competent, eager to do what is good, confident, consecrated, quick to listen, set apart, spiritually discerned, and destined for greatness, you are disciplined. You have renewed strength, wisdom, gracious in speech, an early riser, strong, industrious, and able.

You must believe what the Word of God says because he says that he is not a man that can lie or change his mind. If He says you are

---

[15] John 4:4 The one who is in you is greater than the one who is in the world.

great and prosperous or treasured or his beloved – then you are! Can you see who you are? Can you see who God made you to be? This is your DNA [genetic material]. Who you are is settled according to the Lord.

What you are is a simple explanation, according to the Word of God.

The Holy Scripture says the following:

- You are a joint heir…you share in the Lord's inheritance – it belongs to you as a son of God.
- You are a child of the highest God, the King of Kings. You are royalty.
- He calls you, his friend. You are a friend of God. Treasured, valued, and close to Him.
- You can do more than you can imagine. He gives you vision, hope, a future, and power from on high to accomplish what He's set out for you to do.
- You are anointed. A high honor bestowed from the One Who Is – Jah.
- You are wise, peaceful, and full of God's character.
- You are his product, you are honest, valuable, trustworthy, joyful and a gift from God.

If you trust the Lord and believe who the Bible says you are, whom you are, you become accustomed and eventually "know' this to be your truth. You are wonderfully and fearfully made. You have value, much value! You are worth much more than you allow yourself to believe or allow others to tell you who you are. You are marvelous, amazing and a reverenced creation.

The God who created you, and in you, is a God that never changes. His promises never fail. He remains faithful even when we are not and will always be present.

Even though the Word of God tells us who we are, we allow the world to tell us differently. The world will fill you with ideas that you are of no value – worthless. No value to others much less yourself. The enemy does not value God's gift – life. There are many suicides to confirm the lie that many have chosen to believe. Do not allow your mind to believe such lies – those that are contrary to His Word, His Truth.

You can begin to change your way of thinking, based on the Word by simply telling your mind and settling it in your spirit, what Jesus says.

Do you feel worthy? If you are answering no, why? Most people often do not feel worthy. There are so many reasons that people give to justify such a decision, but the fact is that Jesus tells us all the opposite.

One woman I met was in a "relationship" that was not Godly. She often ranted about how badly her partner treated her and yet she remained with him. She justified staying because of financial need. She added, "and because, he loves me." The evidence was entirely contrary. She put up with his cheating, his alcoholism and as of late, his cursing at her. As time went on, as well as the constant fighting, they had daily, she began to look old and tired. Satan pays his employees with death[16].

She was demonstrating no life in her; she was downtrodden and sad. Her countenance [face] and expression was dejected and unhappy. Her state of mind was taking a toll on her outward appearance as well. She had gained weight, stopped fixing her hair and looked disheveled. She was slowly vanishing from the woman she once believed was worth something. She fell into the lie that is so common among women. She failed to listen to her creator and believed the

---

[16] Rom 6:23 The wages of sin is death

cunning and craftiness of a man who was not Godly. This man who sang her a lovely song and filled her head with lies just to get her to lose the gift within her. He was playing on every need and want she had. Had she only turned to the Lord and depended on Him for her needs and wants, she would be in a better condition and position to receive all that God has for her. So many women fall into this type of lie.

It saddens me that they have no understanding of their self-worth.

They have no understanding of the end result God has for them. They do not believe God can supply all their needs[17]. They are just like "doubting Thomas"[18]. They will not believe in someone who they do not "see". They fall prey and believe in people who Satan uses in his service disguised as a good, caring, and loving person. There are even some who go to church, weekly, who posses these same characteristics and prey on those who don't know their value.

I enjoy paraphrasing Billy Sunday, "standing in a garage doesn't make you a car." Not everyone who says they are a Christian is one! Remember that Satan was quoting Scripture to Jesus. This is why it is so important to identify and understand our worth through the Word of God and not via the world system.

Let us begin by first breaking down the word, worthy. The Lord revealed this to me in the simplest way. The Holy Spirit broke down the word [worthy] for me defining it as questioning value. See the revelation below.

---

[17] Matt 6-31-33 Therefore take no thought saying, what shall we eat? Or what shall we drink? Or wherewith shall we be clothed? For after all these things do the Gentiles seek: for your Heavenly Father knows that you have need of all these things. But seek you first the Kingdom of God, and all His Righteousness and all these things shall be added unto you.

[18] John 20:29 …blessed are they who have not seen, and yet have believed.

Worth [value] + y [why] = WORTHY

Why do you have Worth?

As many revelations from the Holy Spirit are given, they are simple. Yes, simple.

God desires that we know him. He knows that simplicity is better than making something extremely difficult to understand so this was my simple revelation given to me by the Holy Spirit.

We have Worth because it was given to us by the Worthy One, Jesus. We posses value.

So, when you do not feel worthy; you're simply stating that you don't feel valuable and you need to ask yourself – why?

God confirms your worth and tells you why.

God values you. This is evident as stated in the beginning of his creation, you. He calls you worthy. He lays out the many reasons he has given you worth. God thinks so highly of you that He put you in a separate category of his creation above all others. He did not tell a camel to name all the other animals or have dominion over them. He called you to be higher than all His creation. He says, just lower than the angels. He gave you free reign, gave you the right to dominate and a place of position from among his creations.

When a person is esteemed, you are placed in a place of recognition of honor.

God realized how good a creation He made in you, and you need to realize the same. We were made in His image – what an honor to be made in the likeness of a supreme power and divinity. His likeness who we possess his characteristics and love. This is who made and designed you. We have His nature – He is God. He created, and anything that God creates can only be perfect, not lacking in any area. He is God.

Do not misunderstand, we create our imperfections whether in our mind or way of thinking and living or through altering our bodies, but know that once we've accepted His gift [Jesus] then all is made new. We are a new creation in Christ. Amen. For some, it is an immediate and radical change, for others, it is a daily newness a daily determination of accepting the changes being made by the renewing of our mind.

Every day you must solidify what Jesus tells you in his Word about how much He values you. He loves you and treasures you so much that He gave his life for you. Do not undervalue the greatest gift from Him by doubting or not believing in your significance and importance. As you understand your worth through the answering of "why" it is then that your "worth" becomes a fact for your life.

You may ask, how do I lose doubt? By not renewing your mind, daily, that is how. You must believe His Word and execute them into your life. Walking in His Holy Spirit, in the present, daily.

When I think about how much time God took to create man, I thought how wonderful and thoughtful God really is. He took his time to ensure that every hair on your head was placed in just the right place. Even those bunches of hair that insist on going a different direction than all the rest and you have spent endless hours [not to mention hair products] just to make them stay in just the right angle. He knows how many hairs on your head you have. They are numbered by Him. Even when you lose a few, before you know it you have gotten a whole new bunch growing out.

He designed your pores, the hair on your body, every blood vessel, the size of your lungs, your heart and all your organs. He set a timer on how fast your nails grow. He planned out how many fingers you would need to grab and how many toes you would need to stand upright without falling over. He created these odd shapes of eyes that can see even when we do not turn our head [peripheral vision]. He gave us ears to hear and the ability to hear him when no one else can. In his infinite wisdom, God managed to set our body in order to grow our organs so that they can all fit accordingly in our body as it grows. All our organs, muscles, veins, ligaments and blood flow are all synched with the growth of our body. We were created in perfect harmony and syncronized timing.

God gave us the best gift ever, well one of the best; it is the ability to taste.

Oh, how sweet to be able to savor the very things that He created – apples, berries, broccoli, yes, I said broccoli. God created you and me in such a manner that everything works together.

Everything in our body is designed to work for a specific purpose and interact with each other to get something accomplished. He formed your brain to send signals to get the rest of the body to do something. When you feel sad, your heart hurts and your eyes begin to get watery. You find something that makes you happy and your mouth automatically turns upward to create your smile, uniquely. You get angry and your eyebrows point downward, and you get those wrinkles on your forehead and if you continue in this type of negative mind-set, then you develop an ulcer in your stomach. Just think of your respiratory system and how God linked breathing to oxygenating your blood system and then as it travels back and forth throughout your entire body – all day long it becomes your blood pressure that can be monitored to tell whether you need to calm down or get excited! Who else but God could create such a well mechanized system that takes care of itself? He even thought of our skin – regenerating itself so that it continually protects the inner body.

Pores that open and close at the right time, when showering we don't drown because our pores open and close appropriately. They are timed perfectly.

Nerves that send signals of warning, of heat, cold, sweet, sour, and of pleasure. The nervous system sends vast information to the brain and sets off a series of messages to the rest of the body and mind.

You see God thought out every possibility when He created you. He thought of protecting your eyes and added eye lashes. He wanted to protect your stomach so He placed the right number of teeth in your mouth so that, along with saliva, food would be crushed to an acceptable volume to enable it to go down the intended area called the throat down to the stomach where it changes form into nutrients to feed muscles and blood and many other areas of the body. I am so amazed at the vision that only God must have seen the final product – man!

Seeing the end in mind, he gave you internal signals concerning time so that you would be aware of your bodily needs. You get hungry and your mind [and sometimes your stomach] tells you it is time to eat so that your body does not suffer, or your mind does not take on ugly personalities. He gave you the provision for that too in hope that you would opt to happier thought and verbalize them in that manner. Just another reason not to be gluttonous, having an insatiable desire for many things not just for food.

Having precisely thought out our bodily system, He designed it for development – physically and spiritually. Living as our bodies were conceived, we should live in Divine health and happiness.

When God thought of you, He considered all that you would ever need. He thought enough about you to create a well-working body for you. He values His creation – you. If He finds you worthy – who are you not to find yourself worthy? He designed you – what a creator! Enjoy his formidable workmanship. Enjoy how marvelous he made you.

He made you. If He says you are worthy, you'd better accept that and begin to value yourself.

It is when you do not value yourself or believe you are valueable, that you are calling God a liar or stating that He makes imperfect people. He set the standard, not man. You need to reassess those standards that you may be living under. Society does not and should not dictate your value and how you see yourselves.

Bringing value/worth to your mind solidifies what you deserve. Some people think that the only time they should say something great about themselves is during an interview. Wrong! Although it is a great message to relay when interviewing, you should think wonderfully about yourself – always. It is when you begin to find yourself worthy that you can begin to see yourself as God sees you. He loves you.

When that thought of unworthiness comes into your mind – remember that God is not the one telling you that. He tells you throughout His Holy Word, how valueable you are. He made a declaration of His creation, he found it exceptionally good[19]. Realize that those thoughts of worthlessness come from the prince of the air, Satan.

---

[19] Gen 1:31 And God saw all that He had made and found it very good.

You are redeemed and a child of God. Your conversation and thoughts, impressions, imaginations should be of a renewed mind, aligned with the Spirit of God[20].

What I would like you to become aware of is that in the Word of God there are many examples where God has given us, His gift to us, to see how much He really does value us What a privilege we have that Jesus is our mediator, our justifier, and our Savior.

His Word says that we are a sweet aroma to his nostrils.

We are fragrant to him. I know that when I have smelled some women who wear perfume, of not so superior quality, it does not smell all that great and I wonder if they did not know the value of the perfume. I have learned that the better-quality perfume has a higher oil value and therefore is long lasting and has a better smell due to the mix of oils that ferment thus creating a unique smell. The reason that some less expensive perfumes or body sprays do not last long or smell particularly good is because they have an alcohol base instead of an oil base. It is the oils that release the spice, herb or flower that lend to a nicer smell and a longer lasting one.

You are much like that good perfume. You are more costly because God decided to form in you into something that is long-lasting and has an impressive, sweet aroma. It is the aroma of Christ in us that others can smell and see which makes us valuable and worthy. People who can smell and see what you are made of and from can see the worth in you. When we have Christ in us, we have much worth and are found worthy because Christ is worthy – and He is in you[21].

---

[20] Col 3:10 And have put on the new man which is renewed in knowledge after the image of Him Who created him.
[21] Duet 26:18 And the Lord has declared this day that you are his people, his possession as he promised...

You are a treasured possession – cherished, beloved, precious, and valued.

He also declares that you are his, his people – you belong to him.

The birth of Jesus comes to mind when I am reminded that the Wise Men brought the Child of God, gold, frankincense, and myrrh. Gold was symbolic of kingship; frankincense was a symbol of deity and myrrh was used as an embalming oil. Some describe gold as virtue, frankincense as prayer, and myrrh symbolizing suffering. All these are representative of Christ. God valued Jesus, he is the Christ, anointed one of God, his Son. Jesus is part of the triune God, he is deity. Lastly, Jesus was given myrrh a proclamation of his death and his suffering on the cross for you and me.

But what the oils given Jesus have in common are, they are a beautiful fragrant aroma. They are very unique smelling and quite soothing, and a beautiful sweet smell.

When God made you in His image, he made you with an intention.

He made you to be in relationship with Him. He values you and like that sweet aroma, you are costly and you are of great meaning to him. Are you allowing your heart to believe? Can you see and understand that you are worthy? I pray that you receive this revelation that God would have you grasp today.

The Word of God goes on to remind you of your worth[22]. What God has called you, you should not call yourself any differently. You are indeed what God says you are. Realize that Elohim, the all-powerful creator, who created all and is always everywhere – created YOU.

---

[22] 1Pet 2:9 But you are a chosen people, a royal priesthood, a holy nation, a people belonging to God, that you may declare the praises of him who called you out of darkness into the wonderful light

You must be aware that those who do not really know who you are and how much you are worth will always tell you that you are so much less. Words can hurt the moment you begin to accept them into your spirit, into your life. The moment you make them your reality is the moment you begin to believe those words.

When words are spoken, they are sent out for an intended place or person. When our ears and spirit hears them, we have the choice to accept them or rebuke them. If those words are contrary to the Word of God, do not accept them. If those words are not a blessing to you, reject them.

When we speak the Word of God, our ears and spirit hears and accepts them to our spirit.

Therefore, God's word bless us.

In the beginning, as an example. You must speak life into yourself, speaking your blessing. You must also speak it aloud so that your spirit will "hear" it and then your mind will begin to "believe" it.

This is the power of the tongue"[23]

Appreciate yourself, be thankful and grateful for the unique way you look, the individual way that you alone are. There is no one else like you because God sees the uniqueness of you and wants everyone else to see it too. You are God's gift.

As an attempt to reduce God's word, the world produced an approach that many would find a positive one. They have labeled it "positive affirmations." Teaching that by affirming one's positive attributes, daily that the mind would soon have a "new" way of thinking. This is all fine, but your positive attributes need to be established on His

---

[23] Prov 18:21 The tongue has the power of life and death.

Word. This is the attempt the world has made of watering down the Word of God.

God has given us many verses that we can focus on, telling ourselves those truths. Do not give into a watered-down version because that is what the result will be...watered-down. It is unfortunate that these teachings are being led by many behind the pulpit. They are guiding positive messages so that many will "feel" good about themselves. It is good to feel good about ourselves but feeding our mind with worldly theology [religious not relational studies] will bring a worldly result.

The Word of God cannot ever be less than. It is living water, flowing, never-ending, and truth. Consequently, the result of feeding our minds with His Word will result in a Godly renewed mind and spirit.

Each day will result in increased faith in His Word, a closer relationship and understanding, physical/emotional/spiritual healing and a greater awareness of His mercy and grace.

As an identical twin that I am, Jesus helped me to see that DNA [genetic material] is not the determining factor of who I am or what I look like. Although I share the same DNA, I do not share the sameness. I am who God made me to be. My twin has a great similarity in looks but I am still different.

We are not alike because God created me separately and four ½ minutes earlier than my sister.

So even though medical science says that I am the same as my twin, it is defined as identical. God tells me I am unique one-of-a-kind a unique possession and a chosen race[24].

I have learned to value my uniqueness and know that I am a separate person who is wonderfully made. What I share, my DNA, is only a physical trait not my spiritual creation. My likeness is in the physical and not in the spiritual. Because I was created in His image, my worth is derived in my faith in what my Heavenly Father says I am and what I look like [internally].

Many people who do not value themselves is because they may have been told from the beginning not to think so highly of themselves because it's a form of boasting. If you say you are great, valuable, wonderful, beautiful, and that you are worth being heard, then people tell others [or you] that you're conceited, or all puffed up about yourself.

Here is my thought on this:

If God says I am all those things that I have read in His Word, then who am I to argue with God? He must know who I am; He made me!

Now do not misunderstand, I am able to believe that I am a product of his perfection because of Jesus. What God made was a replication of his character through Jesus. If I have Jesus in my life, if he is my Lord and Savior, then I am a reflection of him. Amen.

This solidifies the fact that God took his time when he thought of creating man. He knew that we would all "look" different, but His

---

[24] 2Pet 2:9 But you are a chosen generation, a Royal Priesthood, a Holy Nation, a Peculiar People...

intention was that we would all have the same value [worth]as he placed in Adam and Eve.

I am those things. I am beautiful, I am worthy, I deserve the best, and I have a future of blessings and prosperity in my life – spiritual, mental, physical, financial, and emotional.

I choose to believe that God is telling me the truth of what I can have and what I am to be.

He says that I am the head and not the tail, therefore I lead. He tells me that I am blessed coming and going; time and location are not an issue. He is given me a future and a hope because He knows me and knows my beginning and my end. He is my lamp unto my feet, clear direction that is illuminated so that I am not blinded. His promise is that I will never be put to shame; as a result, I have no reason to fear indignity. I am built on a solid foundation because He is my rock, I will not be moved. He is solid and strong.

He guides and comforts me; it is what completes me. I will bear much fruit; I am a producing positive created being. I am a positive results-oriented woman.

He tells me that I reside under His tent, and I know that the stakes are driven deep so that I am secure and covered [protected]. I know that Jesus says that I am a bright light that illuminates the darkness, and it is consumed by the light within me. I also know that I have the ingredients that cause things to be preserved, things that need to be seasoned. I am the salt that cleanses, purifies, flavors, and preserves. I know that Jesus directs me in the way in which I should go because he cares for me. He has anointed me to preach the gospel to the poor, to bind up the brokenhearted and to proclaim freedom to the captives.

I know that he refines me and makes me pure, presenting me spotless unto the Father. These are all truths that I can draw from daily and as often as I want to or need to. I can expect to be treated with favor. I can expect to be blessed.

I can expect much because God is my provider, and He does not keep back from me. On the contrary, he wants us to receive all he has.

He will not keep secrets; he reveals them all as we seek and ask.

I can expect much because he loves me and everything that God does is for my benefit.

God loves you so much that your dependence on self-worth should and needs to be based solely on the one who knows you best – your creator God, your Savior…Jesus.

Not too long ago, I observed a beautiful woman who was grocery shopping with a man about the same age. This man who was clearly engaged in a conversation with her became loud and began cursing at her, not caring who heard him.

She remained calm and didn't respond back to him but was clearly distressed and embarrassed at what had taken place. No one said or reached out to her, implying not wanting to get drawn in or "get mixed up" in her troubles. I seized the opportunity to affect her life, as Jesus desires that we do through empathy and sharing His good news. Soon after I explained that she was deserving of love, peace and respect and asked her if this man was her husband. Through tears she responded that he was not but that they lived together. There was the first problem. Rather than give her any more of a verbal beating, I engaged her into a conversation about her worth and the possibility of her rethinking who she was according to the

Word of God. Many people are so occupied in their own lives that they fail to pay attention to those that are in their path needing mercy, grace, love…needing Jesus. As we continued to talk, I told her more about Jesus and how she needed to find the pathway that He set out for her. How she needed to see through the eyes of Jesus to see herself as He does. There was more to the conversation, but the objective that we should all follow is that opportunities are openings that the Lord creates for us to present/introduce Him to a much-needed individual whose life can be saved and changed in that very moment. We have the ability to give the gift of God to those who are in need of it, freely.

Therefore, it is important to find what the Word of God says to become more informed and aware because God does not want anyone to perish or be destroyed for the lack of knowledge concerning Him. Seek wisdom thru his Word and continue to draw from it – feeding your soul, your spirit and your mind and allowing the Holy Spirit to place you in that specific lead-in position for those who are lost and in need of a Savior, Jesus. This is what I envision He and Adam would speak about, as they walked in the garden. God always shows us His intent and gives us the way to follow it.

This woman was lost and disconnected to her lifeline, the vine. Her life was being destroyed and she was not even aware of how the enemy was doing it. As is his job description, his M.O. [method of operation].

Satan's job is to kill, steal, and destroy. It was evident as I saw this woman, the Lord showed me her joy was stolen. She was allowing this man to destroy her spirit, her self-worth. Because she was choosing to live, unmarried, she was separating herself from the blessings pre-arranged by God.

She already had thoughts of death as being a better alternative than the life she was presently living

But Praise the Lord for His mercy and his great love towards us so that he gives us the choice to start over. To live according to His plan, to receive ALL that He has set aside for us. Glory to God.

The Lord needs us to stay connected to the vine, to Him for sustenance. His M.O. [method of operation] is quite opposite than that of Satan.

He loves us. He produces our "beginning" so that we can find nourishment where we lack. Just as a child is given milk to start his/her growth, we are fed through our linkage in Jesus, the vine. Isn't it amazing that the grape vine produces a sweet fruit? Whether the vine is an Ivy, Wisteria, Star Jasmine, or Hydrangea, they all continue to grow and do well with a lot of sun [Son]. Interesting right?

We must be like the vine, which staying tied [connected], we continue to be fed, we continue to get strong and aware of whom we are, in Christ. This enables us to continue to grow and sprout. Sadly, not knowing His Word, she was choked by the weeds or severe cuts to the vine where she was no longer connected.

Scripture tells us that there is nothing that is hidden that will not be revealed. The Holy Spirit revealed the lack of self-worth, the lack of peace, joy and most importantly, love in this woman.

This was an opening for either the enemy to win as we say and do nothing or an opening that is taken and life is given that has a future and hope in Jesus. The introduction of life over death. When a piece of the vine is cut, we can water it, give it sun, and graft it back into the main vine for life and new growth. The foreword of a beautiful beginning for a blessed life in Christ. And through progression of His desire, maturity, with good-bearing fruit through the seed that was placed in us.

It is the true understanding of my self-worth that has confirmed his love for me. God gives because it's His nature. Simply, he loves us. He loves his creation. His outcome is as he planned for us.

If God loves you…who could ever love you any greater? His original thought[s] were love towards you and remains. His love is everlasting, from generation to generation.

You see God loves us so much that he takes time to show us all the possibilities available to us. He sets all our blessings right alongside our daily walk as he is next to us every step of the way, ensuring that we recognize them and seize them. Even if we miss them, He makes sure that the opportunities come back our way. We have just got to take the time to recognize his gifts to us and take the time to receive them. We have a father that loves us so much that he continues to see us only one way – righteous. His mercy endures forever. Amen.

And as one who has been blessed, He created you so that he could give you the earth and all that is His…this is a gift that we can freely give to others who are in need of a never-ending resource of love, peace, prosperity, and so much more.

When you become aware of the desire to have "someone" in your life, you start looking. You begin to look with your eyes and flesh instead of allowing the Holy Spirit to show you. When you are in tune with the Holy Spirit because you have surrendered your life to Jesus, it is then that you can move in the direction that the Holy Spirit has planned for you. Who you decide to become closest to you is the person who determines the product of your life. The Lord already knows your life and who should be in it or not. Whatever relationship you decide to create will either be made with the guidance of the Lord or by yourself. That relationship can either be beneficial spiritually to you or be a hindrance to your life. There are many determining factors in which you should center a decision on.

Thru the Word, God gives us those reasons in which we should or should not move into a relationship. God initiated relationship on purpose and with purpose. You must make up your mind to enter relationship with someone who you can relate on a common ground that is centered on Godly values[25]. Entering a relationship, whether friendship or otherwise, with someone who has the interrelated goals you yourself are seeking. Goals and values such as spiritual growth, purposeful divine precedence, primary thinking to do everything with a spirit of excellence [as unto the Lord], always wanting to add value by building in the relationship to develop transparency with one another and with the Lord. Can you relate to him/her because he/she is a fruitful, virtuous, and a person of integrity? Do you see Jesus in their life? The ability to recognize those people that God has brought into your life or those whom the enemy has placed to distract or distance you from, is what will preserve you or destroy you.

How then can you make those distinctions? Look at their track record, ascertain what they've said and/or done, learn their inner values, what is their purpose in life, what is their foundation of belief, where do they want to take you spiritually, emotionally, and are they willing to preserve intimacy with you and the Lord [26], [27], [28].

---

[25] Amos 3:3 Can two walk together unless they are agreed?

[26] Matt 7:15 You will know them by their fruits.

[27] Prov 27:17 As iron sharpens iron, so a man sharpens the countenance of his friend.

[28] 1Cor 15:33 Do not be deceived: "evil company corrupts good habits."

When you are coordinated with the Holy Spirit, you clearly "hear" the Spirit guiding you regarding that person.

Worldly people like to call that an intuition or a gut feeling.... This is a worldly definition, removing the truth which is the Lord speaking to you through the Holy Spirit. Remembering that the Holy Spirit is NOT a feeling but instead the Holy Spirit speaking to your spirit. The Holy Spirit guides. The Holy Spirit will guide you away from a relationship that has no solidity, unstable, and primarily unfounded by the precepts of God. You must recognize who you are and acknowledge who you are not. Is this person adding and building or subtracting and destroying the foundation you have established with the Lord? Simply ask yourself, is this person drawing me closer to God or pulling me away from Him?

The enemy is very subtle, sly, devious, and artful. Examine why this person has come into your life. When you place your life entirely in the hands of your Savior, it is easy to expect answers to your questions. Giving him his rightly position, placing God as your head, your leader, creates the ability for God to instruct you and guide you. As you knock, he begins to open the right door[s]. People who come into your life are never just accidental. God is a visionary God. He is a God of purpose. His plans are set as are his blessings for those that obey and harken to his word. It is when you listen [harken] to his Word that begins the process of bringing action to the blessing waiting for you. Listening is a great and difficult course of action.

If you listen well, you can hear the many excuses some people make why they do not have a relationship with the Lord or choose not to go to church to listen to the Word of God. Excuses never bring results.

No fruit, no desire to know the Master.

This is what you must hear. Listen to the warning[s] that the Holy Spirit gives you regarding those that come into your life. Some people feel it's alright to have those types of people in their life. People who do not desire to know the Master and surrender to him aren't people that you need to associate with.

My mother used to tell me as a child, "show me your friends, and I'll tell you who you are." It did not make much sense then, but it sure does now. I did not even know that she was giving me a biblical principle as noted in[29] the Bible. People find no harm done in having them as a "friend" but, you open the door to disproportionate connection. If they have no real desire to receive the message and the things of God, then you accept them as is and continue an unbalanced relationship.

God was very firm when he met the woman at the well. He did not sugar-coat anything he told her. The choice was given, in kindness yet with firm proclamation of who he was and what she must do. He established who she was and what she must change to be righteous. Fortunately for her, she listened and realized who he was. Her life was changed, and she declared to many, to seek him.

God gave us the example of balanced relationship when he gave Adam, Eve. God knew they needed to be balanced and have the right connection. We come across many people in our life that we need to speak to them about the availability of Christ and his righteousness. It is our commandment to offer them the gift of salvation through Jesus. Because of the change in our mindset, we can offer them the same opportunity to change their conviction. This is the word of our testimony. Glorifying God in the process. We must love them like God loves us.

---

[29] 1Cor 15:33 Do not be misled. Bad company corrupts good character.

It is because he loved the woman at the well that he purposefully chose to speak to her. In the same manner we must love others who are lost, and in darkness, to give them a purposeful life through Jesus.

The Word of God says that we shall know them by their fruits [or none thereof]. Examine why they have no fruit. Is it lack in the knowledge of the Word? Is it just an excuse on their part not to put an effort in knowing the Lord? What role do you have in their lives? Why are they in your focus and path?

You must never take the presence of someone in your life as indifferent. Your indifference can be the determining factor in losing your relationship with the Lord. Listen to the guiding voice of the Holy Spirit. If they are non-bearing, fruitless individuals because their priority is not the Lord, then do not alter your belief with theirs. Be the impactual person they need. Pray for them, converse with them about your faith and don't succum to their ways and thoughts. You have heard the message. You understand the difference between light and darkness. You cannot walk in both light and darkness[30].

I used to worry about being too harsh about telling people about the Lord or thought it was ok to have a friend who had no desire to know the Lord and just accept them as they were. Knowing now the gravity of friendships/relationships, I now continue to feed them the Word of God and leave them with the choice of receiving or denying Jesus. I offer them the gift of God, they can either accept it or not.

For those who want to repent and receive, I support them. I present the Word and am available to share the Word of God and allow the

---

[30] 1John 1:5-6 This is the message we have heard from him and declare to you: God is light; in him there is no darkness at all. If we claim to have fellowship with him and yet walk in the darkness, we lie and do not live out the truth.

Holy Spirit to guide me for their growth. We are all called to disciple and care for them, they are our family of God. Always praying for their understanding and covering through Jesus. Many have distanced themselves from me because of their lack of concern and indifference in the Word of God, in Jesus. I recognize that I have a duty to tell them about salvation, about Jesus and let the Holy Spirit minister to them. Their decision to accept or not is simply that, their decision. I make myself available if they need prayer, have questions they need answers to, or simply want to discuss Jesus. I continue to ask the Lord to send mighty warriors to minister to them and open the door that they may receive Him. Understand that those that the Lord has placed in our path, we must lead them out of darkness, comfort them[31], and always pray for their salvation. This was the role Jesus took with his disciples. He formed relationships with them, taught them, and then encouraged them to do the same with others. We are commanded to love others, we are commanded to give them truth, to draw them unto Jesus. When you place the focus on others and focus on them with love, then the opportunity to have Jesus in the midst is an understood factor.

Because Jesus is love. He has given us the most honest definition of love throughout all the Bible[32]. God has instructed us how we aut to love. He has given us the example of how to love and He has defined love for us.

---

[31] 2Cor 1:3-4 ...the Father of compassion and the God of all comfort, who comforts us in all our trouble, so that we can comfort those in any trouble with the comfort we ourselves receive from God.

[32] Cor 13:4-8 Love is patient, love is kind. It doesn't envy, it does not boast, it is not proud. It does not dishonor others, it is not self-seeking. It is not easily angered, it keeps no record of wrongs. Love does not delight in evil but rejoices with the truth. It always protects, always trusts, and always preserves. Love never fails.

What is more evident is that God has provided us with the wisdom and knowledge of who He is [Love]. Once we accept that insight, we can accept that we also possess that same type of love. When we accept and begin to develop the essence of His love then we become loving in the same manner as God. Let me emphasize that we are not at the same level as God, but we must strive towards the goal of loving as He loves us. The core of the Lord is Love. As we accept all that the Lord has for us and begin to adapt to His love, then it is when our core begins to change into one that is recognizable and unique. This becomes something that the "world" will see as different and hopefully be desirable to them.

This is that gift they will eventually desire.

Understanding that the world may react differently to love because they do not understand true love. The world has defined love as a "feeling" rather than a part of who you should be.

Love is not something that you turn off and on depending on another person or situation. The world has distorted the definition so that love becomes more a feeling than a definition of who you are. God loved us and set the example. He sent his only begotten son to us[33], out of the love He has for you and me.

The word of God gives us various meanings as a teaching that we can learn to develop and more importantly, convert towards.

Love is tolerant. We ensure that we remain good-natured, un-complaining and most importantly, that we remain understanding.

The Lord defines love as kind. In these times that we are in, kindness is a forgotten trait or characteristic within some people. We are to be kind to others, loving them with gentle, thoughtful, considerate,

---

[33] John 3:16 For God so loved the world that he gave his one and only son...

humane, and in a charitable manner. Being patient and emotionally tempered not allowing us to become easily angered. Never being jealous or resenting someone else's success but desiring that they continue upwards toward increase in their life [spiritually, mentally, physically, emotionally, and financially]. Oftentimes this may be the hardest display of love, but it is a big part of following the mandate God has given us. It is actually easy to desire and honestly pray for someone's success when you understand the meaning of the love that is inspired by God.

Now the next part of the definition of love speaks of not boasting. This has a noticeably clear implication. It is used to warn us that we are not to "toot our own horn" or to get into that position of conceit or self-importance. When we boast about things or someone but keeping God in the first position, then it is not boasting but rather glorifying him.

Love will never disgrace or humiliate. It will never bring shame privately or publicly. This is true about that person who wants physical intimacy before marriage, telling you that it is ok because you "love each other". This is veiled "love." If you disguise "love" and are defaming yourself or another – it is not love.

Remove the veil that does not allow you to see clearly, preventing spiritual clarity.

God knowing our sin, still loved us. Never does the Lord humiliate us and once we ask for forgiveness, he forgets our sin. He does not hoard it over us – we do! Just like the Lord, we should not mention something from our past sin if it is forgiven – we should not record mistakes just to bring them up while angry. Love puts past wrongs in the past and wipes them from our memory.

God who is Love, loves us always. Jesus being our example of eternal love, sacrificial love, never-ending love.

God has entrusted us to be in a place of protecting those we love – allowing them to trust and have an awareness that brings a sense of security. When in sin, you are separated from God and open a way for the enemy to come in. When you do not fall into sin and remain obedient to God's will, you will find yourself safe and absolutely loved with no fear but only a sense of oneness. Knowing that you will take care of others as you would value yourself, compromise with sin is not permitted.

With no thought of allowing harm to come to you and therefore not allowing anything bad to come to others. Godly love draws you closer to Him and wants others to draw closer to Him also.

What a grander gesture can we make in love by that of giving others T R U T H. Giving others the chance to know truth, to bring them out of darkness [sinful acts or sinful life] so that they can know Jesus. But to know him through his Word not through your opinion or thoughts. That is the true meaning of love. Loving others in truth.

And lastly, love never fails. The Word of God does not say love sometimes fails or love may fail. It says, love NEVER fails.

I personally received this direct order from the Lord when I was on my way [on a flight] to pray for my sister in the hospital in another state who had been given a report of death. The Lord gave me this Scripture. He clearly said, "Love never fails."

It was later that I saw and understood what exactly He meant. Initially he showed me that I could not fail my sister, since I had Jesus who is love, in me. I had to do whatever the Lord asked of me, to show her love in whatever form it took. Love being displayed thru prayer, truth spoken from the Word of God, having patience, having a serving attitude, and most of all putting her in a place of importance before myself.

Unknowingly, I was later given the most valuable gift. The Lord showed me how love never fails in a much deeper sense. He used me to show her love, but he showed my sister a greater love – Him.

He did this by not failing her. The pronounced death sentence via diagnosis, given her by doctors and believed by her and those close to her, was proven to her by giving her life. I had been told to come quickly [I was in another state] because she was given 2 weeks to live. She had already been in the hospital for 1 week. I panicked and arrangements were made, and I took a flight out the same day.

On that memorable flight from Texas to Arizona, I remember the scriptures that the Lord gave me for what awaited me in the hospital with my sister, family, and friends. He had given me Scriptures that began in Genesis and ended in Revelation. Knowing that most of my family and friends did not really study His Word or seldom opened the Bible, the Lord was instrumental in how His Word would be delivered. He organized the method of conveyance and not until it was all completed, did I really see how loving and compassionate the Lord was and is.

I was instructed by the Lord to request as many bibles we could gather in the hospital. Once we gathered bibles, in the hospital room where my sister was, I asked that we have "church." I began to give the first Scripture which was in the book of Genesis. I proceeded to lead with other Scriptures until we arrived at the book of Revelation and read the last Scripture designated by the Lord. What had transpired was something that only Jesus would have thought of doing. The Lord had made it so simple to go through the bible with many Scriptures and not cause anyone to be embarrassed because they could not find the book and verse because of their unfamiliarity to the bible. It was so amazing, that all those in the hospital room, that all they had to do was keep turning the pages of the bible to the left. It was easy to get to the next book and verse by just turning pages until they came to the specific Scripture. No one had to "search" or look at the index to find which page the Book was at and then find the verse. Everyone was on the same level at reaching Scripture without embarrassment or confusion. Doing this was a testament of His love towards us.

His love was demonstrated as I saw how faithful, how merciful, compassionate and caring he was then and still is now.

It did not matter that no one else saw his demonstration of his love, it mattered to me to see it once again as His truth to who he is. He demonstrated love as a defining word of action. This is a testament of his love and how we are to love one another. Love requires an action that defines Jesus [he is love].

This is the action that confirms His Word [34]. Knowing Jesus, makes loving one another easy.

I had asked everyone who was in my sister's hospital room only one request. I stated, "if there is anyone who is not in agreement that [sister's name] is NOT dying, please leave the room until we are done. Sadly, there were some that left the room. But I knew that God had plans so I rested in the faith knowing that God had purposed that His Father be glorified. As I proceeded to quote Scripture, being an obedient vessel, I began to see my sister's gray skin turn to a healthy color. Death had no authority because we were speaking life. Our words [Scripture] had a destination and the target was my

---

[34] Isaiah 55:11 So is my word that goes out from my mouth: it will not return to me empty, but will accomplish what I desire and achieve the purpose for which I sent it.

sister's death announcement. Scripture, the LIVING Word had to take the place of the report that was not given by God. As "church" was nearing a close, as hyped up on drugs to have my sister semi-coherent that she was, she managed to say "Hallelujah" and give an Amen at the end of church.

At the end of the week, we did not take my sister to hospice, as planned, but instead took her home. It is there that during our alone time, my sister and I discussed and shared the Word of God. I remember her asking me one time that I was in deep meditation of his word, she asked me, "is He speaking to you?" My response was, "yes." I read her Scripture that was for her and her healing. I asked her if she was ready to surrender her stubbornness and allow God to be her Master, her Teacher, her Guide, her All-in-All. Her response was YES! I read her Scripture [35] and explained word-by-word, she fully understood and was excited that she had made a decision that would change her life.

I continued to read and explain [disciple] to her in as much as time permitted. Praise the Lord that he timed everything, and visitors did not interrupt our time of prayer and study. I took her to her Chemotherapy treatments and began to see His work. The therapies were a mixture of three distinct types. The Oncologist began to lesson from three types to two then 1 type until on that awesome day...

I remember when her Oncologist made a comment to me, she said, "I don't understand this but whatever you're doing keep doing it because her cancer is no longer active". Her husband, her daughter, and I were present at this medical visit with her Oncologist.

---

[35] Rom 10:9-10 If you declare with your mouth, Jesus is Lord, and believe in your heart that God raised him from the dead, you will be saved...

My response was easy. I told her that the Lord had not failed my sister, that he loved her so much and He had plans for her. To my surprise, the doctor commented that she understands that there are no scientific explanations but that she knows that there is a God that does what science cannot do or can be explained.

This is the unfailing love of God. This is why Scripture says, love never fails.

But beware.

For those who have a misguided interpretation of love and attempt to lead others in redefining love, beware.

Attempting to lead others through self-gain and sin will only keep you in darkness and separate you from God.

This is the vital portion of the meaning of love that is so necessary – love others in truth. Truth is Jesus' word. The word is Jesus' love speaking to us.

Jesus is love. Simple fact. This is a simple moral method of living.

Living righteously and full of love. It is when you are in relationship with the Lord that you have a clearer understanding of love and can love someone as Jesus loves us.

It is when two can agree on this meaning of love that they can walk together[36].

Understanding love, the love in fullness as described in the Word of God has multiple blessings.

---

[36] Amos 3:3 Do two walk together unless they have agreed to do so?

This is a gift from God and provides us:

- The blessing of knowing God's love
- The blessing of being able to love.
- The blessing of loving together as one with the Lord.

This is a reproducing gift. This gift is not tabooed to re-gift.

God has given me the ability to see and understand his love. Soon after I gave birth to each of my children, he allowed me to see what some may take for granted – a healthy baby. I saw more than the obvious ten fingers, ten toes, a completely formed body and an alert baby who seemed complete. This was obvious. What I later saw as the excitement of finally delivering a child, was the true gift of life.

God allowed me to see the greater gift. These individual babies, had been formed in his image. I was blessed with children who were happy and protected.

My children are blessed, happy and protected. The Lord showed me my worth through them. He allowed me to see how much he cared for me by the love that I received back from them as I held them soon after delivery. They were created, just like he had intended. It was then that I realized their worth and mine. He loved me so much that he gave me children who I could care for and love as he has cared and loved me, following His example.

There is nothing that can compare to the creation he made in my children and then blessed me with my grandchildren to show me the next chapter of my life.

They although vastly different in personality, they are blessed with special talents and gifts. As adults now, I can only continue to pray that they see, accept, and understand the greater gift of God in them as they continue on their own road and destiny. My first child has the ability to change the mood/setting of a room once she enters it. Her attitude, personality, and strong-willed sense makes the difference in what takes place as she enters a room. My second child has a passion that stems from the gifting of the Lord. The Lord has given him dreams that when acted upon, bring prosperity and positive results. My youngest child has the patience to think things out before speaking. She has always had a quiet spirit and one of thoughtful consideration. Sweet, soft, and beautiful is the definition of her spirit.

My children now adults have separate lives that they have been challenged with. They have walked roads going in many different directions, but I know that their fundamental thinking will keep them focused on the right course.

The road and destiny that the Lord would have us travel oftentimes has forks in the road. Some people may consider them to be stumbling blocks or obstacles. I prefer to see them as gifts from God. You see when the Lord allows something in your road of life, it can be something that will get you closer to the goal. It can be an opportunity for growth, or a closer walk with him. Not all things that are amid your life are lessons. Sometimes those things that make us pause are meant to make us pause. Pondering what the Lord is saying or showing us is a formidable gift that comes from him to us through relationship and transparency with him. Sometimes he will show us something through his eyes so that we can see with and in his love any given situation as his gift to us. This kind of relationship is something that everyone should desire. I say desire because many times the Lord gives us gifts and we turn them down or fail to ask for them. I desire all good gifts from God. As he bestows them on me, I rejoice just knowing that I received a "gift" from God. Amen.

THE GIFT OF GOD

As my grandchildren grow and live their lives, I do not falter in my desire for them to know Jesus at a higher and intimate level. My heart's desire is that they too fall in love with the Creator, the Almighty, Son of God – Jesus.

You might wonder what are those gifts that the Lord gives us…

To some, those gifts take on a very meaningful part of their daily existence. One example might be the necessity of good health to a single parent who needs to take care of his/her child[ren]. The basic, for them is nothing more than good health for sake of providing for someone other than themselves. This gift will enable them to do what is necessary with no need for anything else until the next issue. To some a basic need not believing for the bigger gift. To some this same gift is a crucial need that is fervently asked for and desired. A critical need and desire for someone battling a terminal disease that has torn the hope of futuristic goals and desires left a hopeless scene in their minds and even in their heart.

This simple gift for someone who sees a means to an end seems a minor request and oftentimes becomes a standard just to get the day done.

Now to that person who has been handed a death sentence/report, this gift from God becomes central in their faith. Some have even believed that one can bargain or deal with God to obtain this gift. They fail to see that it is a GIFT! The Lord reminds us that he is a gift-giver and all we are required to do is ask and receive. He is more than able and surely willing, to give us the simplest to the most unforeseen possibility of ever receiving [in our minds] some of his gifts. Let me explain. Some people are determined that it is okay to pray and ask for something when it is nearly impossible or too big and begin to really hope that the Lord "will" grant their request. They will miraculously begin to do all the "right" things, pray, fast, and even tell people of their re-gained faith in hope of receiving his gift. For some, that is a good thing [as Martha Stewart would say it]. Some have regained their faith in having hope in the Lord. For others it's more of a help me now, and I'll try to get to know the gift-giver, later. The unfortunate thing about those who only seek the Lord when they need something that they themselves are unable to do, is that they do not really ever understand the magnitude of His gift[s]. I have learned that I can come freely to him and ask for his gift[s] whether big or small and know that he will not withhold to those that will glorify his Father in Heaven because of it.

Simple piece of wisdom I received when I had a ridiculous headache that was making my body ache and changing my mood. I realized that instead of reaching for a pill that was intended to relieve pain in your head/eyes/sinus…I needed to reach for the great physician who had a better method of relief. I reached for Jesus. If he was able to heal the sick [heal as in remove], then he was able to heal my silly headache. We need to create a new found faith that if Jesus could heal the most difficult of situations or health issues, then those other "little" health problems are easier to demonstrate their healing. Simple thought process. I realized that this simple concept was a part of the "knowledge" that he tells us about in Scripture [37]. This is why it is so important that we seek him through his Word. He desires that we understand, rather, that we know him. He desires that we be in relationship with him so that we know what his will is for us, to know what he has made available for us – freely. Part of knowing who my Redeemer is, is knowing that he first loves me. Because he loves me, his will for me is to increase me in Him.

Increasing me with his manifested blessings. Divine health, financial opportunity to bless others, mental stability, emotional security

---

[37] Hosea 4:6 …my people are destroyed from lack of knowledge…

and of course, spiritually filled [daily]. He wants me to have greater ability to spiritually be in a dimension that is Holy Spirit led.

Being Holy Spirit led and being in a total state of surrender to the Master of your life and having a real understanding of the Master of your life is what moves you into that dimension to enable you to see things in an absolutely true Spiritual sense. Having an understanding that Jesus IS your Master of your life is crucial in enabling the Lord to fully guide you and help you to stay on the path that has been created just for you. When we allow Jesus to guide us and we surrender to the Teacher, we set ourselves up to receive all the good gifts He has already given us. It is when we truly know that the greater is in control and is in us that we can begin to see things spiritually and in another dimension. The Lord wants us to continue to grow spiritually and to have all His gifts added unto us [38]. We must begin to desire and seek the domain of God. Understanding not where God lives but understanding his kingdom is the scope and span of what He is all about, the life of God.

It is when we pursue, go after, work towards, and try to achieve finding His scope of life... or as defined by Merriam-Webster dictionary:

> the realm in which God's will is fulfilled.

> a realm or region in which something is dominant.

> an area or sphere in which one holds a preeminent position.

...that we understand that the kingdom of God is not a place but rather a status in which you place God in your life. It is accepting

---

[38] Matt 6:33 the kingdom of God, and his righteousness; and all these things shall be added unto you.

that God holds that position of exalted and paramount rank where no one else could ever hold, it is allowing the Spirit of God to move within your life and allowing God's will to shift our way of thinking and causing a refocus of living.

As we allow and re-shift our way of thinking we place ourselves in a position of agreeing with his righteousness. Discerning his will and his righteousness, we place ourselves in a position to receive his virtue, morality, justice, decency and honesty, blamelessness, blessings, and all his gifts. It is then that he attaches all these things to your life. This is the gift of God to you.

This is the dimension that we can walk into to see and receive his gift of healing, for one.

There are more gifts of healing than just the healing of health. There is the healing of finances, emotional break-through, newness of positive self-esteem, mental wholeness, spiritual awareness, and mental stability as your thoughts become as his thoughts.

Pursuing the anointed one of God, Christ Jesus will get you to the place of understanding the gift of God.

Understanding that the gift of God brings us to a place of healing by believing and in continuous pursuit of him. This is why I reach for Jesus not just in the trivial things but in the massive things too. Headache to Lupus, I pursue Jesus and find my gift.

It has become a truth to understanding on some greater level, or dimension, why so many people remain in an unfit state and yet continue to wait on God.

Wisdom – understanding things that most people cannot understand – comes with and through the relationship with the Lord. As you are more involved with the Lord, through His Word allowing His Word to be alive in you, you allow the Holy Spirit to teach you and help you to grasp the meaning of connection with the Lord. As you continue to associate and stay connected to the Lord, you move into a place of greater understanding [wisdom] of His Word – of Him.

Being able to receive His wisdom is a gift of God.

Unless you have a bond or link it is difficult to understand what the Lord's will is for your life.

The link that God created, yes created, for us is his son Jesus. This is why God made the statement [39] that Jesus was the only mediator between us and God.

There is no other link, connection in which we can obtain His gifts.

Wisdom enables us to comprehend his will and puts us in a position of knowing what his righteousness is.

God intended, through Jesus, which being in relationship with him we would recognize and identify with him. This is how we can receive his gifts – identifying with him. Not to say we take on his identity but rather to realize his identity and strive to abide in and follow his example. Adhering to his way and remaining in his will.

Remaining in this position or way of thinking and living we place ourselves in a place for receiving all his gifts.

We oftentimes will only receive some of his gifts not because the Lord withholds them but because we choose not to get them.

---

[39] 1Tim 2:5 For there is one God and one mediator, between God and mankind, the man Christ Jesus.

We are told when we are noticeably young not to be selfish and not to take in abundance. How odd that we are taught from an incredibly young age not to do that instead of being taught about the idea of what giving is all about. Giving and receiving gifts.

It is not a method to boast of your ability to give but rather a method to boast about the Giver Himself. Through Jesus' desire to see you blessed, He provides the gifting ability to enable you to bless others as you are blessed. It brings happiness knowing that you are in position to give as you've been given. It is the opening of the windows[40] that pour out blessings that enable you to share of those blessings. It is a gift-giving gift!

Not everyone understands the inference of blessing/gifting others. The significance is that we, a valuable thing, be a delight to others. The Lord has something in mind besides blessing/gifting you. In providing a blessing that overflows, you are in position to give from the abundance purposefully and positioning yourself as the extension of the Lord. Others will see His greatness and understand the blessing of being gift-givers; hence bringing glory to the Father. You are perceived in a positive light that causes recognition of the one who positioned you for greatness, favor, and to have influence on those in need.

Not all gifts are material. The anointing, spiritual gifts given to us by the Lord are not intended to keep to ourselves.

These spiritual gifts are for the building up of the church. Some of these gifts are specific to someone who may need a word from the Lord for direction, edification, or confirmation.

---

[40] Malachi 3:10 and see if I will not throw open the floodgates of heaven and pour out so much blessing that there will not be room enough to store it.

It is marvelous how the Lord will use me to gift someone with a Word specific to his/her unspoken need. It is through my obedience to the Lord that the receiver can "hear" an unanswered request/prayer evidence of the reality of the Lord in their lives. Many people will ask, "how did you know?" My response is always the same – "I didn't, but the Lord heard your cry and has seen your heart." This is a gift to them. If I did not remain obedient and listen to the request of the Lord, receiving his gift [Prophesy] then I would not be able to give the gift from the Lord to the intended receiver.

Consequently, the gift of God continues from one to another glorifying our Heavenly Father. As we follow the example of obedience from Jesus, as he demonstrated throughout his life, we are in position to continue that resolve – *giving* - the gift of God.

As we follow, we must ensure that we are in the position that God purposed for His gifting. Simply said, be obedient, listen to His direction and place yourself where He leads you. Listen to His instructions and then be ready to see Him work! Praise the Lord Almighty!

Another area where God's gifts are given to us is through prayer.

First, prayer is not something you recite and repeat and repeat and repeat, stand up, sit down, kneel and repeat.

Prayer is open communication between you and the Lord. You communicate to him [verbally] and listen for his response.

As defined by Merriam-Webster dictionary:

Communication: The act or process of using words, sounds, signs, or behaviors to express or exchange information, ideas, thoughts, feelings, to someone else.

So, let's examine the process.

1. Use words.
2. Use sounds.
3. Use signs or behaviors.

Prayer involves the use of words and sounds so we must speak.

You may use words known as language familiar to you whether English, foreign language or spoken in the language of Tongues through the Holy Spirit. This involves vocalizing your words – speaking to them aloud.

These sounds spoken are audible but may be a familiar language or unfamiliar as in the gift of Tongues which is speaking in the Spirit[41].

Prayer may consist of signs or behaviors such as prayer by way of dancing unto the Lord as David danced. This is not a rehearsed dance, but one done in the Spirit as unto God. The behavior of prayer may be whaling or a cry from a heartfelt place, sadness, hurt or even cries of intense thankfulness which words cannot express.

Prayer is not rehearsed nor seeks approval from others [42]. Prayer must be earnest, it incorporates worship and seeks God.

Jesus gives us an example of how to pray when he recites, famously known as, the Lord's prayer. Let us examine this prayer.

---

[41] 1Cor 14:2 For anyone who speaks in a tongue does not speak to men but to God...Mark 16:17 "And these signs will follow those who believe...they will speak with new tongues." Acts 2:4 All of them were filled with the Holy Spirit and began to speak in other tongues as the Spirit enabled them.
[42] Matt 6:7 And when you pray, do not keep babbling like pagans for they think they will be heard because of their many words.

First Jesus begins by acknowledging our Father [we must admit, recognize, accept, and confess that God indeed is our Father].

- Our = Greek= hemon meaning us or we
- Father = Greek; pat-ayr literally father or parent

He then continues by acknowledging his role and place, his position, and his residence.

- Which = ho he to; the this that one
- Is in = Greek; en primary preposition denoting a fixed position
- Heaven = Greek; ouranos the same as the sky, as the abode of God, air

Jesus then proceeds to define God's name.

- Hallowed= Greek; hagiazo to make Holy, purified, consecrated
- Be thy = Greek; sou of thee, thou, thine own
- Name = Greek; onoma called

He continues to confess God's place as a King and confirms desiring that his rule or reign enter [come or be set in us]

- Thy kingdom = Greek; basileia a realm, reign, that is where his royalty rules
- Come = Greek; erchomai enter, go, grow, resort or be set

Surrendering himself to the purpose of God and not his

- Thy will = Greek; thelema purpose, decree, pleasure [inclination]

Agreeing with God that as he desires it to be.

- Be done = Greek; ginomai to cause, brought to pass, partake, pass, be performed, require, come to pass, be made, fulfilled

Declaring where we are – our place, domain, person's surroundings.

- On Earth = Greek; ge soil, by extension a region, ground, land, world, country
- As in = Greek; hos in that manner, like, as unto, as it were
- Heaven = Greek; Ouranos the same as the sky, as the abode of God, air

Jesus gave us an example of where we can begin to have conversation with him, our God. He thrives on having a personal conversation with us for our well-being, not His. We must understand that through this method and time of "prayer" we are placed in a specific position where Jesus is our primary focus, and our will goes by the wayside because this is about Jesus and not ourselves.

Prayer, as set by Jesus' example, must begin by confessing that we know who he is and his rightful place in our lives. It is when he is placed first and we remove all our selfish reasons for "talking" to him that our prayer is received as something good[43], a sweet aroma as is incense.

Just imagine when there is a sweet aroma that surrounds you, it immediately puts you in a peaceful, happy and state of euphoria [bliss].

It would be hard not to smile or feel joyous, right?!

---

[43] Psalm 141:2 Let my prayer be counted as incense before you

Just imagine this is the result of prayer. We are pleasing to the Lord when we pray.

But there are also other reasons to pray. Praying or meditating on him brings strength and increase of faith. Prayer should not be done just when we are in need or want of anything but rather it should be done at every opportunity we have.

The benefits outweigh the losses when you pray.

You see prayer to the Lord takes on an especially vital role between him and you. He regards prayer highly. The Word of God tells us we can boldly approach and have access to the throne room of grace[44].

He takes them to the Holy of Holies. This is the place where He listens to our prayers. A special place set aside for just this one thing – prayer.

Understanding that through repentance of sin, allows prayers to be heard and answered according to His purpose – His will. God keeps his word, his covenant and recognizes our hearts and our humility. Our humility comes from admission of our need that is greater than our ability, and that we need His help. We pray most oftentimes at request of him intervening in the specified situations we voice through prayer. Prayer is not only communication of requests it also should be an activity we incorporate in our daily lives. As we continue the habit to pray, we begin to trust him and understand more clearly that he answers according to his will for our life that unless we trust him, we remain unsure of the outcome of our situations voiced in prayer. Trust is a lot like faith. We must believe what we are praying about has been heard by the Lord.

---

[44] Heb 4:16 Let us then approach God's throne of grace with confidence, so that we may receive mercy and find grace to help us in our time of need.

PROPHETESS GRACE LOPEZ

The magnificent outcome is that he gives us the desires of our heart. When those desires are built and centered on glorifying God, they become that gift that he grants to us. Because he knows us, he gives us gifts that will continue to grow our faith, that continue to grow us in every conceivable way. He adds to the relationship based on his love for us.

As we understand his love for us then it becomes very easy to strive to increase pleasing him through prayer, worship, and obedience. This inherently becomes the reason that his Word becomes real and consequently adds to the desire to know him more. This is what reverence is all about. Having the highest esteem, regard for who Jesus is and for all that he did for you and I and knowing that he continues to remain faithful to us, even when we are not[45].

If you have lost your faith or question your faith in the Lord, is it due to something that was unanswered or from a hardship that cannot be explained? Confess your weaknesses and your need for His help.

Your faith will increase as you continue to seek him, trust him, and accept that even through testing and trials – he will never leave you. The Lord will always hear the prayers of his righteous, his children.

So many times, we ask for something and do not have the ability or trust to wait for the answer. We are under the assumption that we should expect an answer in our timing, which expected time as now. We suppose that God can or rather should give us answers rapidly. What is our thought process behind that? It is not like we are not important to Him and therefore should respond quickly, right? God is a thoughtful God. He is a God of order. Because he sees the result, we cannot understand all the action and effect that an answer has. Our desire is immediate and oftentimes we cannot be patient enough to seek God for the answer. Prayer enables us to

[45] Heb 13:5 I will never leave you, nor forsake you.

see our request at a deeper level and God helps us understand what we truly are asking for and why. That is, if we listen.

Meditating on the Word will help us to listen to what God is saying to us. It will enable us to see him with more clarity.

God took his time to create a world that was full of his gestures for us. We must meditate on his Word to help us to put into perspective what we are asking and why we are asking. It will also help us to understand if this is his will for us or not. How do we know what his will is for us?

Sometimes we think that if something happens or someone tells us something that it was "sent" from God. Whenever that happens, are you confirming that with His Word? If not, then it's most likely not God giving you, His answer. Why do you suppose that it works that way? God is a god of order. He is already given us the tool that will help answer our questions. That tool is His Word. Many will say that He sends his prophets to deliver his answer. That may be true, but you will only be able to confirm that through his words. If you are getting answers from someone that does not give you Godly counsel or Godly answers, then you must question if it is the right answer or not. How could a non-faith-based friendship give you Godly counsel? You cannot depend on answers from people who are not walking together with you [those who do not have the same faith-base]. God will always give you an answer, it may not be one that you want or in the period that you want it in, but He will give you an answer. How you decide to "hear" it is dependent on you.

I continually pray for my children and grandchildren[46].

Hard-hitting, effective prayer is what we are called to do. I know and believe that my life has been a good example of my faith in Jesus

[46] James 5:16 The prayer of a righteous person is powerful and effective.

and as my grandchildren grow up, they can reflect on my many discussions about the Lord and his love towards us.

Many people are accustomed to hearing "I'll pray for you" and feel as if they are just given "lip service." This is so sad that Christians are taken at their word and then fail to keep it.

One of the most important discernments that I've received is the importance of prayer. This is the reason when someone shares some issues or concerns, I ask them can I pray for you. I do not mean later, but rather, now. Walking and doing in the present. Being obedient to the Holy Spirit, actively. These are also doors that you must see opened for you to walk in the divine plan Jesus has for you and this person who is in need! Placing them in a position to receive His gift.

Prayer is not something that we have all been programmed to believe is taught, but rather it is something that is voiced from us to God. It is a method of communication between us and God. Just as God walked and talked in the garden with Adam, it is important that we walk [spiritually] and talk to God. When we talk to him, He really does listen. Oftentimes we are so busy talking that we fail to hear him answering us. He will frequently interject in us his answer and sometimes if we're quiet enough, we can hear his voice in response to our dilemma, question, or interaction.

According to His Word, he has told us that he hears our prayers[47]. This is also a reminder that there are conditions to him hearing us. A reminder that we cannot be in sin and expect him to participate with us in anything outside of repentance. What he treasures most is the ability to embrace our communication with him. Prayer is not just words but is something that the Lord has placed immense value in

---

[47] Prov 15:29 …The Lord is far from the wicked, but he hears the prayer of the righteous.

and treasures it. He treasures our words as a one-on-one relationship. This is the evidence of a father caring for his child.

Those of us as parents, uncles, aunts, grandparents, listen to our children and respond immediately. We do not postpone their need to be comforted. We do not wait to give them a word that will encourage or bless them. We act on their need right away. This is the example Jesus gave us. When he saw a need he acted on it instantly. When he answered prayer, the result was immediate. This is what we can expect as well. Healing of the body, healing of finances, of situations that need reparation, or simply a word of encouragement. We can expect or experience an immediate response. It is when we do not because of disbelief that we cannot see immediate results. Some fall under the thinking that God is not able to perform such requests as they are near an impossibility, and we are not deserving of such a grand gesture. Why would you think such a thing? God is love. He is our Father. What parent would not move mountains to take care of his children?

We need to remove those kinds of thoughts and see God as he is.

He is:

Jehovah-Jireh [God of Provision][Gen 22:14]
Jehovah-Shalom [God of Peace] [Jud 6:24]
Jehovah-Nissi [Lord our Banner] [Exodus 17:15-16]
Jehovah-Rapha [Lord who Heals][Ex 15:26]
Jehovah-Tsidkenu [God of my Righteousness] [Jer 23:6]
Jehovah-Sabaoth [Lord of Hosts][1Sam 1:3]
Jehovah-Shammah [Lord who is there] [Ezek 48:35]
as found throughout the Old Testament.

Jesus, in his obedience never to be greater than His father, he brings our prayer requests to a special place and to Almighty God.

God thinks so highly of you and me that He tells us that he takes our prayers into the throne room. The Holy of Holies is the place where He listens to our prayers and gives them to our Heavenly Father. He displays value behind what we have said to him whether in thanksgiving or in pain. The spectrum of our needs, questions, or simply thanksgiving communicated to him brings honor to his place in our lives.

How many times have you desired something great for someone? You voiced it to them and still felt that there could be more to speaking a desire for them. When we talk to Jesus and tell him that we understand his place in our lives and ask in total honesty and in goodness for something/someone, he listens and weighs it to see if this lines up to the provisions and plan for you. Jesus is a giving God and desires never to withhold something good for you[48], according to His will.

There are many teachings and scripture of prayer in the Spirit. This is a sacred method to communicate spirit to Spirit. But in this epoch period of interaction with one another, can we not find words to express our thanksgiving, our immeasurable feeling of gratitude? Can we not find the words to articulate our concerns, confusion, happiness, sadness, heartache, or thoughts? We are so programmed to use icons, or emoji's instead of words that we have lost the original method of communication – speech.

We can go to any store and find a card that expresses what we would like to say to someone, whether it is for a birthday, holiday, get well wish or sympathy. While it is an innovative idea and usually is received well from the recipient, it is someone else's thought[s]. We purchase the card because it's what we intended to say or it's what we're thinking. This is where the communication element of voice

---

[48] Matt 7:11...how much more will your Father in heaven give good gifts...

is so much sweeter. We're able to interject our voice to relate the true message we want someone to "hear" from our voice, our heart. Therefore, when we pray, thru voice to Jesus, he hears our heart. When we are appreciative for all that he does for us, or when we are experiencing pain, he hears us. Yes, he "sees" our heart, but he spoke to Adam...he walked with him in the garden.

Some people recite and state that God knows what we are thinking before we ask. While that may be truth, we still are given the example to "speak" and ask. We know what our children need before they ask but if they never asked would you know if they genuinely wanted or needed anything or if they wanted feedback from you? Communication is the method that God used when he walked and talked in the garden with Adam. Communication as defined by Merriam-Webster, is a process by which information is exchanged between individuals through a common system of symbols, signs, or behavior, a verbal or written message.

As most of our communication should be personalized when speaking to a loved one, we speak to our Heavenly Father with verbal or speech [speaking] using our known language or spiritual language.

Some customs pray in silence...this is not the custom that Jesus provided for us. He gave us the foundational method for us to begin to understand the meaning of prayer. The Lord's prayer gives us the clear understanding of prayer and the elements required to give honor and praise through prayer. Let us delineate the example he provided. He said, "and when you pray, **say**" ...Our Father [addressing specifically God our Father] which art in heaven [recognizing his place], hallowed be your name [reverencing him as he is holy], your kingdom come [requesting his reign on us]. Thy will be done [His will not ours], as in heaven, so in earth [with us presently]. Give us each day our daily bread [asking him to provide for us]. Forgive us our sins [as we repent], for we also forgive everyone who sins against us [following Jesus' example to forgive] and lead us not into temptation [help us to do the right thing], but deliver us from evil [protecting us, recognizing his status as our Savior][49].

Once you understand the foundational example, then your ability to convey your thoughts and heart to him is easy. You begin to express, with words, your gratitude, reverence for Him, and acknowledging to Him that he is your everything. You can begin to understand that when you pray, requesting something, that it is based on His will and not yours. It is easy to understand that every thought he has for you, is according to His will and intent for your life. It is an invitation to bless you and do it in abundance. I can only imagine how happy the Lord is to hear from us, continually seeking a more intense and deeper relationship with him. When he hears our requests, he is excited and willing and wants to bless us with more than we could even expect or think of [50].

His instruction to his disciples was, to "say." We must give utterance, put voice towards our prayer. For the spirit within us to "hear" we must speak into our spirit to confirm what we are asking or stating. We also must understand that when we speak or utter we are sending those words out to fulfill a designed place. When accompanied with the Word of God, His Word will not return void.

Prayer is essential to our relationship with Jesus. It is the foundation in which we begin our journey of salvation and life everlasting. The word of God clearly makes several statements about prayer. One of the most powerful is this scripture found in Isaiah 59:2 [but your iniquities have separated you from your God; your sins have hidden his face from you so that he will not hear.] God because of

---

[49] Luke 11:2-4 And he said unto them, when you pray, say...
[50] Matt 7:11 ...how much more will your Father in heaven give good gifts to those who ask him!

his holiness, cannot be in the midst of sin. Jesus cannot bring your prayer into the holy throne room. Hence, prayers of a sinful man are not heard from God. God will hear the prayer of a sinful man when done in the spirit of repentance[51]. This is again another example of "voiced" prayer. Speaking your faith into salvation.

We may be praying in a spirit of thanksgiving, making a heartfelt request, or conveying an act of repentance through prayer. Our spirit will confirm and receive the prayer and know that Jesus is acknowledging these words. Our Lord will then speak on our behalf to our Heavenly Father in the throne room, the holiest of holies. As our ambassador, justifier, he submits our requests to the Father.

Prayer is powerful, effective in bringing life changes, it is the evidence of your faith, and demonstrative of the continued relationship that you have with your Savior, Jesus. Amen.

Let us not misunderstand, just as he knows our heart and mind, he may not answer our prayers. He hears them but may not answer them because he knows what is best for us and will not do anything contrary to His Word. It also may not line up with the plans and purposes for our life.

Oftentimes we may get discouraged or give up on the belief that God is not going to answer our requests. What we ought to do is meditate on the requests being made and see if it lines up with the Word, see if it will bring glory and honor to God, or if our prayer is beneficial to our life and testimony of God.

---

[51] Rom 10:9-10 If you declare with your mouth, "Jesus is Lord," and believe in your heart that God raised him from the dead, you will be saved. For it is with your heart that you believe and are justified, and it is with your mouth that you profess your faith and are saved.

Spending time in meditation with the Lord will oftentimes clarify this for you. We begin to realize if our requests are self-serving, nonessential, selfish, unglorifying to the Lord, or the opposite.

I have found that when in quiet meditation, in the word of God, I hear more clearly. The Lord may give me a specific word, a vision, or put a specific person to confirm His word to me. It is not by coincidence that a brother or sister [fellow believer] will just call me or be in contact with me and have the exact word/message for me that I was praying about. It is not that I lack faith, it is the opposite – the Lord confirms that I did hear him and that he wants others to be lifted spiritually as well. It is like a two-edged sword, cutting both ways and creating a sharper edge – both ways. The person who contacts you and gives you the confirmation is also being encouraged that he/she is being obedient by following directions and "hearing" the Lord by giving the word/message in confirmation to me. The Lord ensures that his children are all in one accord. Sharpening each other through confirmation of His Word and consequently edifying building up of our faith. What a blessing it is to know that obedience brings honor to Jesus and that we are rewarded for it.

Our reward is much greater than the world seeks, monetary or self-righteousness. The Gift of God is the blessing knowing that we are linked, connected to the main root, the vine[52].

Prayer, when done with a clean heart, can either close or open a door. When we allow the Lord to continue to guide us, with His plans and purposes for our life, we are allowing him to protect and invite us to receive his gifts. Many will need to have doors shut so that he can open others that have blessings. Frequently God will close a door in protecting us and allow us to see the blessing on the other side.

---

[52] John 15:1-9 ...remain in me, as I also remain in you...remain in my love.

I always questioned why, in scripture, we are told to "move mountains." The Lord gave me the revelation when I was in deep meditation and prayer and showed me that this "mountain" was blocking my view of the blessing/gift he had prepared for me. Once I saw that I had to "move" that mountain to receive the invitation of His gift, I was able to let go and close this door. His desire to protect and bless me was evident when I closed the door and moved the mountain that was hindering me from the invitation to receive his enormous blessing [gift]. I have realized that the plan of God is so much bigger, better, and comes with such peace and joy that I try to always be faithful in moving those mountains and unblock – releasing my blessings. I also can see those mountains clearer and am continuing to learn to see them and know that I have the ability, thru Christ, to move them out of the way.

When we begin to see with clarity, we can also allow Christ to light up those dark roads of the unknown and trust God that he will light the pathway[53] of blessings and security. Once we have a lit pathway, we must walk onto that path into our divine blessing set for that appointed time. Following and surrendering your life, allowing the Lord Jesus to guide you will ensure that the plan and purpose he has for you is manifesting throughout every decision you make that is being guided by the Lord.

You must allow yourself to trust and follow the lead of the Lord. He will never guide you in the wrong direction. He will never set you up to fail. He is a God of promotion not demotion.

He always increases in you, he will fulfill the gifts and anointing within you. As he blesses you, he enables you to bless others. In doing so, we can exalt and give honor to our gift-giver, Jesus.

---

[53] Ps 119-105 ...Thy Word is a lamp unto my feet, and a light unto my path

Prayer is his gift to us. He does not require that we communicate with him, but he honors those who choose to do so. He knows what we need before we even ask.

Prayer is effective and provides the resolution to many a quandary of issues and questions. The Lord will give us so many opportunities to spend time with him, but we frequently miss them. We become too busy, replace free time to use it for something or someone else, or simply just choose not to take time out for him.

But there are also other reasons to pray. Praying or meditating on him brings strength and increase of faith. Prayer should not be done just when we are in need or want of anything but rather it should be done at every opportunity we have.

The benefits outweigh the losses when you pray.

You see prayer to the Lord takes on an especially important role between him and you. He regards prayer highly. The Word of God tells us we can boldly approach and have access to the throne room of grace[54].

He takes them to the Holy of Holies. This is the place where He listens to our prayers. A special place set aside for just this one thing – prayer.

The magnificent outcome is that he gives us the desires of our heart. When those desires are built and centered on glorifying God, they become that gift that he grants to us. Because he knows us, he gives us gifts that will continue to grow our faith, that continue to grow us in every conceivable way. He adds to the relationship based on his love for us. As we understand his love for us then it becomes

---

[54] Heb 4:16 Let us then approach God's throne of grace with confidence, so that we may receive mercy and find grace to help us in our time of need.

very easy to strive to increase pleasing him thru prayer, worship, and obedience. This inherently becomes the reason that his Word becomes real and consequently adds to the desire to know him more. This is what reverence is all about. Having the highest esteem, regard for who Jesus is and for all that he did for you and knowing that he continues to remain faithful to us, even when we are not[55].

If you have lost your faith or question your faith in the Lord, is it due to something that was unanswered or from a hardship that cannot be explained?

So many times, we ask for something and do not have the ability or trust to wait for the answer. We are under the assumption that we should expect an answer in our timing, now. We suppose that God can or rather should give us answers rapidly. What is our thought process behind that? It is not like we are not important to Him and therefore should respond quickly, right? God is a thoughtful God. He is a God of order. Because he sees the result, we cannot understand all the action and effect that an answer has. Our desire is immediate and oftentimes we cannot be patient enough to seek God for the answer. Prayer enables us to see our request at a deeper level and God helps us understand what we truly are asking for and why. That is, if we listen.

Scripture tells us that if we ask it will be given to us[56]...we ask through prayer. The Lord wants us to "ask" to have a conversation with him. As our Heavenly Father, he wants to "give" us our requests. Now just like an old TV program, "Father knows best" that was out many years ago, our Heavenly Father knows best so sometimes what we "ask" for we may not get, or our request may be delayed. He knows our plans and destiny, so he makes the right decision whether he

---

[55] Heb 13:5 I will never leave you, nor forsake you.
[56] Matt 7:7 Ask and it will be given to you; seek and you will find; knock and the door will be opened to you.

grants our requests, delays it or not. He contours what we ask for so that it will work into the designed path for our life. This is why he can tell us that we can expect to be prosperous, that his plans will not harm us [or our future]. The Word of God goes even further to promise that he is giving us hope and an opportunity for a future[57].

It is important that as we "ask" that we also listen. You must begin to enter a quiet state and be still in his presence, in his worship, in reverence. By entering meditation this is the process that will enable you to "hear" him.

Meditating on his Word will help us to listen to what God is saying to us.

It will enable us to see, in part, his desire for our life.

God took his time to create a world that was full of his blessings/gifting for us. We must meditate on his Word to help us to put into perspective what we are asking and why we are asking.

Meditating will also help us to understand if this is his will for us or not. The Holy Spirit will help us to understand and guide us in the process to obtain wisdom in what we ask and why.

If he bases his decision to give us what we ask according to his will, how do we know what his will is for us?

Sometimes we think that if something happens or someone tells us something that it was "sent" from God. Whenever that happens, are you confirming that with His Word? If not, then it is most likely not God giving you, His answer. Why do you suppose that it works that way? God is a god of order. He is already given us the tool that

---

[57] Jer 29:11 For I know the plans I have for you, declares the Lord, plans to prosper you and not to harm you, plans to give you a hope and a future.

will help answer our questions. That tool is His Word. This is why it is so important to meditate and keep his word in our mind, daily, often. Keeping his word within us is not a trained process but rather a lifestyle. Ensuring that the Word of God is what we begin and end our day with. Thinking of Him, on His Word, and what he is saying to us through his Word.

Many will say that He sends his prophets to deliver his answer. That may be true, but you will only be able to confirm that through his word. If you are getting answers from someone that does not give you Godly counsel or Godly answers, then you must question if it is the right answer or not. How could a non-faith-based friendship give you Godly counsel? You cannot depend on answers from people who are not walking together with you [do not have the same faith-base]. God will always give you an answer, it may not be one that you want or in the period that you want it in, but He will give you an answer. How you decide to "hear" it is dependent on you. Keep in mind that the world system will provide you with a lot of choices or counsel you in a manner that will satisfy you and whatever situation you may encounter with an answer that most likely will make you feel good. Not everything that makes you "feel" good is necessarily the right answer. It is important that you obtain Godly counsel or ask the Holy Spirit for wisdom, knowledge, and confirmation.

Many of us know our parents. We can guess, when asked a question, what their answer may be. We can almost expect the response because we know how they think or believe, what may motivate their answer, or just because they have prior experience and believe they can provide a good response and their counsel is sound [or at least it "sounds" good].

It is to our benefit to find out who Jesus is, to find out what he wants for us, to learn his characteristics, and match his desires for us to allowing those to become a part of our life. Making the time for him takes fidelity and diligence. In these times of microwavable thinking and living a free-spirited lifestyle with no moral compass, it is difficult to commit to changing for a God who has thought out our life and wants us to take the time to follow his direction. In following the direction and being obedient to the Lord, we are walking against the grain of this world structure. Because of this, we are labeled and ridiculed, targeted, and harassed. In the great scheme of things, this is in no way a comparison for what Jesus has done for us. He gave up his life for you and me. He took on our sins, bore our sickness and was chastised for our unrighteousness. Through him we received the Gift of God – Jesus. Amen.

Jesus continues to show his children, favor, his faithfulness, and love. He showers us with his mercies, his grace and over and over, his love. When he provides this, he gives us the means and the ability to do as He has instructed us in following his example. Throughout his Word, he shows us what we are to do, say, and be.

I was told many years ago by my first pastor, that the Bible stands for basic instructions before leaving earth.

I understood that indeed the Bible is an instructional tool to follow as a written word directly from my Savior but what I later learned is that this inspired Word of God, in written format, is more than an instructional tool. It is a life-giving word directly coming from Jesus.

His word is life, it is alive. As we recite and receive his Word, it is breathed into our spirit providing life to our soul. When we receive it as such, it becomes manifested in our life. His words are a means to speak to us individually and to provide us with instruction so that we follow the path that he has laid out for us. He wants us to walk out our purpose, to follow in the direction that He has set out for us. His plans and purpose for our lives will bring us to our destination, not only on this earth but with Him in everlasting eternity.

Unlike plans that we receive from someone else who may be in authority, those plans have a timestamp and reach a conclusion, an end.

With God, his plans have an eternal result.

Jesus knows our end result and is faithful to see us reach that outcome and in the process, we obtain more than our original thought that began our reason for asking...

As a father may plan for the future of his children, our Father also has set out a plan for us. There is of course an enormous difference between our earthly father and Father God.

Plans made to end in completion of a worldly system have a finite destination. The reward for completing a goal or plan is rewarding but only for a period of time. Many people move from one goal or plan to another whether or not they complete the goal or not. Their reward is often short lived. God's plan has a determined destination. This plan he has for us does not end because of worldly rules but instead are infinite because he is an eternal God. His plans are set in order as we follow his directions. As he lights our paths, and we in obedience follow, we move from glory to glory. Simply stated, he moves us from triumphant honor to triumphant honor enabling us to bring praise to a righteous God, Jesus. His plan for us is attainable and the reward for completing the race is eternal. His determined plan for us has a purposeful result. The Lord is you might say, a results-oriented God. He plans out our destiny/destination and the road to complete it may come with trial, adversity, and hardship but the result is tangible, full of value, and we can grasp the revelation of the struggle in obtaining the result. His proven results are designed to bring us to our intended destiny/destination that always has positive benefits.

Through Jesus we may receive promotion, a higher level of devotion, a greater level of revelation and of course a solidified understanding of his love. He does not withhold from us; his reward is his free gift to us.

The world system comes with ties, what-ifs, bartering, and requirements that do not equate with the cost that it may have taken to reach a goal or plan.

Our Father rewards us for simple obedience and a trustworthy attitude and commitment.

The word of God throughout gives us examples of our Fathers' character, his integrity, and his ultimate love. When we examine, believe, and surrender to live and do as unto God, it is then that we begin to find out who He is. He will advocate for us, protect us, provide for us, enlarge in us those qualities and gifts in us for our benefit and for others to receive as well, he fills us with his qualities as we choose a surrendered life to Him. It may seem that the request is great but when we choose to follow and accept Jesus, it is easy to desire the things of God. The reward is tangible and obtainable, daily. His plans and purposeful decision to bless us is a decision that most of us as parents make without thought. We understand that rewarding a child with love for being obedient creates a loving child. We must train them as we also continually accept being trained by God. When we make that decision, we surrender to His will and not ours. We accept the plans and purpose he has for us and follow the GREAT shepherd. He is the one who guides us with his staff, ensures that we do not stray or get lost, and makes provisions for a fulfilled blessed life. As the GREAT shepherd, he cares for his flock. He ensures that we are safe, that he provides for us, and that if we stray, he is quick to bring us back to a safe, secure place where he will put us back on the road where our destiny/destination is prepared. It is in the obedience in following Him and the plans set forth that we can achieve the goals that lead us towards the level and position of his esteem.

God is the only one that does not have a selfish intention for our blessed life. He is a true loving father who wants to give us good gifts, who desires that we come to the fullness of a secure and blessed life. Frequently we find that man will want the best for us and will even assist us in setting a great goal, but their motif may be somewhat skewed or full of envious intent. Everything that God provides and gives us is done with love as a father would possess the same intent for his child. The world system has taught us that when we gain and obtain a goal that the credit is always due to someone else. Achieving a goal is always reflected and deflected towards someone else. It is something that is designed to ensure that the credit is given to someone who has not fought the good fight but rather instructed and pushed for you to accomplish it, then take the credit for your success with no payoff for your willingness to follow along. God on the other hand, his desire for you to reach the goal has rewards that put us in a place of receiving and not in a place where we are deceived by the trophy that gathers dust. God assists us in following the path which enables us to continually receive...his blessings, his favor, his strength, his wisdom, and so much more. Even when we fall short of the race, he picks us up and re-directs us so that we can achieve the many blessings along the way as we strive to finish the race and receive our reward.

There are many opportunities to "win" a great big house for free, or so we believe from the many contests and propaganda available to us. There's ALWAYS a "catch" involved.

Some may say the same about accepting Christ. What he promises does not come with fees or unattainable requirements. He simply asks that we remain faithful and follow his instructions for a life that is made available in abundance.

As a Christian, I often thought this was going to be hard to follow. Surrendering to His way of thinking, and doing as He instructs, changing my lifestyle or way of thinking – I really thought it would be so difficult and for a moment debated the result and if there was any worth to the greatest gift.

I must admit that I struggled to allow someone to dictate my life. I soon found out that following Jesus was easy because he made the way. He set my life up with blessings, he taught me lessons about so many things, he did the impossible for me. It was easy to surrender my life to a life-giving God. It was easy to trust him. He asked for my obedience and faith/trust in him in exchange for an abundant life full of truth, a means to a destiny eternally with him, and a life full of his love. This is the actuality of his word[58]. No one or no other "god" can make this statement. Because we are lost, he shows us the way because he is the way...because he is the truth, he is trustworthy and he cannot lie...because he is the life, he promises us eternal life. He is God. Jesus is our Savior. He is our rescuer, deliverer, and helper.

More specifically, he rescues us from evil. He rescues us from eternal death. He rescues us from being lost and saves us. He is our deliverer. He brings us out of the snares of the evil of the world. He delivers us into a place of peace and security. He never leaves us without resources. Our biggest resource that He's given us is the Holy Spirit, our helper and comforter. In this concept, it is easy to surrender, to let go and fully trust him.

Setting my mind in doing exactly that, surrendering, fully trusting God, has brought me out of places that have been humiliating, hurtful, and even in places of despair.

---

[58] John 14:6 I am the way and the truth and the life; no one comes to the Father except through me..

But with confidence and patience, I have received all the recognition I need and rightly so, deserved. I have obtained that through his Word, through knowing his desire and intent for me. I have found that my life has been set up for success and not failure. I can fully trust the Lord to keep me in peace, safe, and loved – unconditionally. As I meditate in his word I find that he's preparing for me greatness, that he is providing me with all the necessary tools and resources to put me in a place where my life will be enriched and for the life of others. He has set me up to find within me all the good that he created in me. As I have laid down my life's struggles and pain, he enriches my life and my soul with a love that is immeasurable and inconceivable. No one or nothing can quiet my mind or heart like he does through his Word.

At my lowest point in my life when I was raped, I was able to fall into my Heavenly Fathers' arms.

He held me and quieted my spirit. He loved me and helped me to see through His eyes. I was able to see how I could find the ability to forgive because he forgave us and laid his life down for each one of us. I began to heal and eventually was able to understand that because my violator did not know Jesus, who is Love, he was not able to understand what love was. What he saw in me was my love, the love of Christ. He misunderstood what love really is and forced his way to obtain his version of his understanding of love. It was his way of getting love, one way or another. It was extremely hard to get to that place of forgiveness, but I also knew I could not enter the same place of taking from someone, like he did. Hatred and bitterness was not a fruit I could have in my life. I fought hard not to bear that type of fruit, toxic and poisonous.

He took what he believed would bring him love. God showed me that I and no one needs to take from someone. God freely gives his love to us. It is well with me as I have chosen to forgive and pray that he will surrender his life and know real love, to be in position to repent, enabling him to receive the gift of God.

Those who knew what happened had a tough time and were terribly angry. I had to bury my anger and let God oversee that situation, cleanse me from any hatred, and hurt. My God is a just God and most importantly, is a loving God. I often am amazed that I did not enter a mindset that would harm me or others. I realized that my God would give me justice and that he would restore all that was stolen from me.

In the process of staying under the protection and love of Christ, my heart was made soft and pliable again. I knew that Jesus was restoring who I was and gave me a greater understanding of people who are lost, who don't know the love of Christ, and ultimately, he restored my understanding of my value, my worth. I had believed that because of what happened to me, that I had no value anymore. I had thought that I was a damaged person and knowing what happened to me, someone would see me as a damaged product.

It is through the commitment to stay in prayer, to meditate on his Word, and to trust Him, that I was able to find that the Lord had restored in me who he created me to be. As I learned later through God's Word, I lost nothing. He restored me and gave me a greater level of love towards the lost, the hurt, the ones who felt they had no value or worth. I began to be amid many people, men, and women, who had similarly gone through the same circumstances. Every day the Lord chipped away at the brokenness and put me through the fire to create in me a newness and a greater understanding and compassion for those who felt lost and worthless. Just as a potter forms and refines his product in the fire, the Lord begins to recreate[59] removing the cracks made up by lies and hurts. While

---

[59] Jer 18:4 But the pot he was shaping from the clay was marred in his hands; so the potter formed it into another pot, shaping it as seemed best to him.

going through the process, the Lord produces a new product that is free from impurities and evidence of hurt and pain. During my healing, the Lord began to create in me a new love. He orchestrated divine appointments where I was able to minister to someone who was trying to "deal" with the same type of loss and pain.

I understood their grieving. Something was taken, stolen and grief took over. Because of the love that I was engulfed with, through Jesus, I was able to minister to others. I was not aware that I could have such empathy and compassion to extend to those who were experiencing such sadness and turmoil – such grief. The fear, anger, confusion, loss, and hurt that I experienced became less as I began to minister to those who were dealing with the same hurt and anger.

I can honestly say that I experienced so many levels of things.

I had such anger, such shame, felt lowly and at fault. God, through his Word, allowed me to understand Him at so many new levels. I really understood his scripture that says, "you meant evil against me, but God used it for good" [Gen 50:20]. Satan will always fail because God is greater. God was able to use what happened to me and used it for good. I can minister with the intent that God-breathed in me, forgiveness, mercy, and wisdom.

During the process God was able to restore my joy and brought me back to who I was before what had transpired. God's Word took on greater levels of realness, of life. His Word restored every part of me and brought me a new joy. Every day that Jesus filled me with his love, I was able to continue to see the bigger picture to see the reason Jesus surrendered his life for us.

As a physician desires to bring his patient back into a state of health and sound healing, this is where the Lord brought me to. I entered an understanding and place of healing that enabled me to not harbor hatred or any mal intent towards my violator. As the many years have gone by, it is easier to understand that Satan's MO [Motive of Operation] is of course, to kill, steal, and destroy. Knowing this through the Word of God, I was able to speak life into my spirit. God restored me. Satan was not able to kill me, kill my spirit. He was not able to steal my joy, my value and integrity. And lastly, Satan was not able to destroy my life. I understood that God had a purpose for my life and moved in me to fulfill that commandment to be his instrument. In the end, Satan lost again.

I am a new creation in Christ. Praise God. In Christ alone I found my joy again, in Christ alone I regained my value. He gave me a new strength and knowledge of who I am according to the Word of God. I know above all that Greater is He that is in me, than he who is in the world [1John 4:4]. Amen.

I relied on His Word, solely. The world told me that I was damaged, that I would have PTSD, fear men, fear surroundings, and that I had to accept that my anger and fears were normal. What a lie! This is not normal. What the Word of God showed me who I am is my norm. God didn't tell me that I had to accept negative characteristics of myself due to what happened, he on the contrary has seeded in me all the deep truths about who I am and no one can change that.

I did not fall into the lie, that some people tell themselves, " Hi my name is ____ and I'm an alcoholic". When the Lord heals, he removes all the disease. Our response is Yes [Amen] and we must continue to believe and remain faithful. This is the same stance I took when I received my healing of Lupus. I chose to put my faith in His Word, in Him, my Saviour.

When in a position and options are available, through obedience in hearing the voice of God, we must always listen to His voice. His instruction is always clear, and his intent is always to benefit our life and ensure that we are in position to receive all that he intends for us.

When you hear his voice and go and do as he commands, it's easy because he knows you and always has his best interest in you. He knows the way, the path that he has put you on. You can trust him because you are walking with him. Wherever that path takes you, you are never alone. He is with you directing and orchestrating all the things that will enable you to get to where he is leading you. Take his hand as a child takes the hand of his father. Fully trusting without fear or concern. Walking by his side. You may go down a road that may curve to the left and then take you to the right. The pathway is all thought out by the Lord and what you may encounter can be a lesson, blessing, or a deterrent. Staying connected and obeying God all the while allowing him to lead you, will take you towards your destined place. You must continue to trust God, being faithful, patient, and obedient[60] with an expectant mindset.

While obeying the voice of God, we oftentimes encounter lessons. Depending on what you may be going through or what the Lord wants you to learn, we end up being taught and obtain wisdom, empathy, clarity, or many other types of knowledge. He may intend to teach you something that you can relate to or gain an increased knowledge on the matter. It may be a lesson that you need for someone that has intended a divine appointment to bring a connection or introduction to our Savior. If you are at a crossroad and in a state of unsurety, God may direct you to a place where he can bring you clarity. Obeying the voice of God and trusting that he knows the plans and purposes for your life, will oftentimes end in blessing and enriching your life.

---

[60] Deut 28"1, 2 diligently obey the voice of the Lord

Not many nights ago, I was awakened at 2:30am. I did not understand why and went to the bathroom and returned to bed shortly after. The next night I was awakened again at 2:30am. This time as I made my way to the bathroom, I realized that God wanted me to intercede in prayer.

I did not know for who or what so I began to pray in the Spirit and then I prayed for my children, grandchildren, ex-husband [who was in bad health], family members, and anyone of which I could think. I spoke binding/losing with authority and rebuked any spoken words against me or curses spoken against me, I took and stood with authority as given to me by Jesus. I returned to bed and slept peacefully. The next day I woke up at my normal time between 5-5:30am and began my morning practice of taking my doggie out to do her business, watering my plants outside, and getting my coffee ready for my bible study time & writing.

About 8:30am I went from no pain to an excruciating pain that was intolerable. I was doubled over and unable to stand, sit, or lay down without experiencing severe pain. The pain was so severe I ended up vomiting three times. The contents of the vomit looked like bile. I began to cry out to the Lord, asking if there was something I needed to have come out of my body, to allow it to come out. I contemplated going to the emergency room and continued to cry out to the Lord. I began quoting scriptures and rebuking the enemy for this attack on my body. I visioned my armor on and any fiery darts aimed my way were bouncing off and going in a direction away from me. I was angered that I was experiencing this pain and asked the Lord to place His healing hand on me and allow me to be healed and I would give God all the glory and use this as my testimony that Greater is He that is in me, than he who is in the world. I spiritually dressed myself in the Armor of God and continued in prayer and praising God for my healing and revelation. I proceed to attempt to shower, in case I had to go to emergency room, and asked the Lord to give me wisdom.

As I got out of the shower, and was drying myself, I realized that the excruciating, unbearable, and foreign pain had left. God gave me revelation about spoken curse against me, so I gave him glory and placed the person who God showed me who was cursing me, placed them at the feet of Jesus. I prayed that they would surrender to Jesus and ask for forgiveness. I asked that the Lord send a mighty warrior to give them a message from God in hope for their salvation. I also forgave them because they are lost and do not have the Spirit of God and therefore do not have the love of Christ. Once I realized my pain was gone, I began to praise the Lord for my divine healing and immediately called several people to testify of God's healing hand on me. Later that evening, the enemy attempted to tell me that I wasn't healed and that the pain would return. I quickly stood my ground and spoke binding and releasing, with authority I commanded the lying devil to go. I continued to praise the Lord and thank him for my divine healing and have been pain free since. Amen.

I know that my faith has been the instrument that allowed me to receive my healing. Regardless of others' lack of faith, I know what the Lord has done for me and I bless His Name. Remaining faithful to God and having all faith, hope and love in Jesus Christ is what has delivered me from the attempts of the enemy. Praise the Lord Jesus! Because I obeyed the voice of God and interceded when he woke me up, I know that the enemy was attempting to derail me from praying/interceding so that he could kill, steal and destroy someone. I was obedient to the voice of God and did not allow the enemy to deter me from the plans and purpose the Lord had for me that morning. Amen for several good reports and answered prayer.

Obeying the voice of God sometimes we think is a deterrent to our life. It may not necessarily come from God. Sometimes we may ourselves create the deterrent or as I like to think of, go off on a bunny trail. We take our focus off the Lord and think that pausing or adding to our path will be all right. It is then that we take our eyes off the path that God has laid out for us to follow, that brings delay and postponement. This is why it is so important to obey the voice of God.

Had Moses not heeded the voice of God, he may not have been the source that God used to free his people in the period that was intended. I am assured that God would have provided the way, nonetheless.

When Moses did not follow God's instruction, we see the result for his disobedience. When we are in relationship with God, we must trust and take heed. We cannot hear his voice and choose what we want to obey or not. We quickly learn that there are consequences for disobedience.

As children I am sure that we all at one time or another attempted to challenge direction from our parent[s]. We quickly learned that for disobedience we received some variation of punishment, which included a lesson learned.

If we take our eyes off the Lord, and do not harken to his voice, we put ourselves in a position for Satan to distract us and deter our purpose or plans. In the Word of God, we find Scripture that demonstrates when Peter took his eyes off of Jesus and he began to sink, he no longer was walking on water with Jesus[61]. It is vital that we "listen" to the voice of Jesus, stay focused, and trust in him always. In taking our focus off Jesus, we allow distraction in.

---

[61] Matt 14:29 ...Then Peter got down out of the boat, walked on the water and came toward Jesus...

Distraction is intended to remove our focus and direct you away from something or someone. When we listen to the voice of God, we must remain focused on just him. As our Father, he knows what we need, he knows the direction we should go but we must trust and accept that he has given us his promise. His promise to us is to guide us, teach us, provide for us, and know that his plans are to gift us through our obedience[62]. The result is a precious gift from God.

Knowing that his intentions are always focused on teaching and blessing his children when we are obedient. This is an extension of our trust and confidence in him.

When we pray, when we listen to the voice of God in a spirit of surrender, we can expect that God will direct our life so that it is blessed, safe, and prosperous. We know that his result for us is one purposed to be full of thankfulness. We can trust that he has our best intention for our life.

Some of us enter prayer at the request of others or on behalf of someone else. Intercessory prayer can be demonstrated like Moses did when he prayed for his people. Moses prayed for those who still had unsurity of what and how God would do for them even though they had concrete evidence of God's love for them in carrying them out of exile to a promised land. Moses also prayed that those faithful would not cease or waver in faith and not succumb to peer pressure. There were those who prayed to the golden calf idol because they put more emphasis on what people thought rather than on what God had said to them.

Just as Moses prayed for his people, we must intercede on behalf of those who do not yet have a solid foundation in Christ and pray that

---

[62] Jer 29:11 For I know the plans I have for you," declares the LORD, "plans to prosper you and not to harm you, plans to give you hope and a future.

the will not succumb to the pressures and believe wholeheartedly in the abilities and promises of God.

In praying as an intercessor, we may enter a prayer of lament. Asking God to forgive his people or for oneself. When we pray, whether for others or ourselves, we must place ourselves towards the place where Christ is – in the temple at the right hand of the Father.

Christ dwells in this Holy place. This is the ceremonial place that Solomon built, according to the blueprint of God, the house of prayer. Prayer is communication with God and is a practice that Jesus gave us as an example. When we pray and listen to the response from our Lord, it is divine dialogue. This happens when you have established a relationship with God.

Some may use prayer out of fear[63] and it is an admission that we know that God is more than able and is the only one who can change an impossible situation.

We come to acknowledge this simple truth from a state of the unknown, fear. Just as a child comes to their parent when afraid, knowing that their parent has a greater and vast ability to comfort and bring resolution to their need [oftentimes].

It is also a good practice to enter prayer early in the morning, at the start of your day recognizing that is through the grace of God that you woke up to another day. It is good practice to do so, beginning each day in thanksgiving[64] and using the example Jesus gave us.

---

[63] Psalm 119:145-146 I call with all my heart; answer me, Lord, and I will obey your decrees. I call out to you; save me and I will keep your statutes.
[64] Mark 1:35 Very early in the morning, while it was still dark, Jesus got up, left the house and went off to a solitary place, where he prayed.

Jesus also gave us another example where he prayed at night. As He and his disciples went to a place called Gethsemane, Jesus said to his disciples, "Sit here while I pray." We see here that not only was it at night, but that he separated himself to talk to his Heavenly Father[65], undisturbed and in private. We ought to do the same, pray undisturbed by influences of other people, television, social media or whatever may take away your focus on communicating with God. Sometimes at the end of a day, after all your to-dos are done, you can spend quality time in prayer where you are not distracted from anything or anyone who can and will deter your prayer time with your Savior.

Whether we pray out of fear, in the morning, in the evening or out of need, lack of wisdom, joy, gratitude, intercession, for those in authority, for our enemies, or in all occasions, [66] Jesus has given us the promise that He hears our prayer.

When we are unsure how to pray, Jesus gave us a model of a simple but meaningful prayer.[67] We need to pray as Jesus did, acknowledge, be thankful, ask for His guidance and then accept that He will answer according to his will. Our attitudes and actions can thwart our prayers.

---

[65] Mark 14:32...sit here while I pray."

[66] Matt 7:7-12 Ask and it will be given to you...James 1:5 If any of you lacks wisdom, you should ask God, who gives generously...Phil 1:4 I always pray with joy...1Thes 5:16-18 Rejoice always, pray continually, give thanks in all circumstances; for this is God's wil for you in Christ Jesus...1Thes 5:25 Brothers and sisters, pray for us...1 Tim 2:1-2 I urge, then, first of all, that petitions, prayers, intercession be made for all people—for kings and all those in authority...Matt 5:44 But I tell you, love your enemies and pray for those who persecute you...Ephes 6:18 and pray in the Spirit on all occasions with all kinds of prayers and requests.

[67] Luke 11:1-3 When you pray, say: "Father, hallowed be your name, your kingdom come. Give us each day our daily bread.

We must ensure that our intentions are not selfish or done in obligation rather than in true intent. Sin can cause God not to answer prayer as well. Make sure that you first repent of any sin or offense towards God before you make your request in prayer. Sin separates you from God, therefore, your sin can cause God not to answer your prayer.[68] Make sure that when you enter prayer, for yourself or others, that you are sincere and have all the right motives in your requests.

As we enter into a state of prayer, in supplication, we can enter with an expectation and knowledge that He will make every decision for our life with an intention and result that is a blessing for us. His intention is to provide hope, gifts, rewards, provision, and continually increasing our faith-base in Him. It is good to pray for rain/showers – your blessings.[69]

There is a mentality that some have taken that God is wanting us to sacrifice. Although his word states that he wants our obedience over sacrifice. Many think that in sacrificing, they are making amends and becoming closer to Him.

Jesus was the ultimate sacrifice. We cannot forfeit anything greater than what Jesus did for us on the cross. The greatest propitiation we could do is to obey the voice of God. In obedience to the Lord, we recognize his faithfulness, we admit our trust in him, we admit that he is our King, our Father, and author and finisher of our life. Obeying the voice of God allows him to be the provider, the true guide, and sole ruler of our life.

It is easy to surrender to Jesus knowing that He always has our best intention for this life on earth and for our life in eternity. As I

---

[68] Jer 11:11 Although they cry out to me, I will not listen to them.
[69] Zec 10:1 He gives showers of rain to al people, and plants of the field to everyone.

harken to his voice, in obedience, He blesses me and ensures that I am walking on the path that he has directed me. God will surround you and place you in a position to bless others as a family, His family.

Just as Moses and Abraham listened to the voice of God and trusted God wholeheartedly, God ensured their lives were set in place for his blessings and for generation after generations.

Both Moses and Abraham had no idea what God's plans were but through their obedience and dependence on God, they walked into their blessings.

Going on the examples that Moses, Abraham, and so many other God-fearing men gave us throughout the Word of God, we see the common denominator...God blessed their obedience.

Through relationship, they were able to "hear" him and listened.

One of the greatest testaments of remaining obedient to the voice of God was noted in the bible about Job. He was put to the test and yet remained faithful to God. The beauty in the end of his story was not all the gifts, blessings that he received but rather the confirmation of the promise that God gave him. Most have focused on what was taken from Job instead of what Job gained, spiritually.

Job never wavered in his faith and trust in God. No matter what was put before him, he maintained his faith in God and the promise made to him. Knowing God and understanding that he loved him, allowed Job to trust him. Job understood that God was God and totally trusted him, no matter what!

Job's reward, for his unwavering faith in God, was beyond what he could ever have or think. This is God. My God does not only provide for us, but he also opens the windows of heaven and pours out such a blessing...[70]

Throughout the Word of God, we have evidence of his gifting as a result for obeying his voice. My God is merciful, thoughtful, and a gift-giver.

His grace and evidence of his love towards us gives us a reason to trust him more. Remain in relationship with him and continue to obey him.

He makes a way where there is none, he blesses us in overflow when we cannot even imagine his generosity. Remain in relationship with him and quiet your spirit to recognize his voice. Be in stillness, not allowing distraction to move you from the position of hearing his voice. Becoming a better listener, we can hear his direction, learn of his great love for us, and begin to see the blessed plan for our life. Once we have mastered this, we will surely begin to hear his voice. Then as Jesus provided examples for us in his Word, we must listen and follow his direction.

Because he is a purposeful God and knowing our destiny, we must trust and be guided by him. We must attempt to see through his eyes. His focus is not the mountain in front of us, but rather the gift behind the mountain.

That gift is no longer in the background but instead is in the foreground. We must not place so much focus on our problems but instead focus on the end result. When we quiet ourselves and listen to his voice, he is already placed us on the path where the mountain is no longer blocking our path, enabling the purpose to become evident.

---

[70] Mal 3:10 ...and see if I will not throw open the floodgates of heaven and pour out so much blessing that there will not be room enough to store it.

Many of us focus on the problem stemming out of fear of the unknown. What we need to do is change our mindset and focus on the result so that our mindset becomes accustomed to focusing on the end result as God sees it. Moving our focus to a result that is of the same result as what God intends is building of our faith.

We must build our mind to retain memory based on end results and not current problems or fears.

Just as an athlete builds muscle memory, we must build our faith. Training our thinking towards the result and not the current problem or situation.

Time and energy focused on the problem does not solve anything. That type of focus is wasted time and diminishes your faith. It begins to question God's intention for us. It also allows for negative thoughts and fear to enter in instead of the opposite of what God's intentions are for us. To be able to increase our faith-base we must admit and acknowledge the problem and then understand that the Lord has a better plan. His plans and purposes for our lives are based on his love for us and to bring us to a place of gratitude and love. When we have the result as a place of hope, we can refocus and see the hand of God in it. He is aware of our situations and problems but patiently awaits our acceptance of his promise and/or gift to us.

We must honestly believe that his intentions for us are pure, loving, prosperous, and beneficial in maintaining our peace and trust towards him. When we adapt to his way of thinking, we can begin to understand how to combat the enemy's plan and replace it with the plans and purposes that he has for each one of us. Do not allow fear to enter your mind, do not minimize what the Lord can do for you. Just because you may find it hard to see the opening of your blessing does not mean it is not there.

The Lord can and will move mountains when you move out of the way and trust him. He says that he knows the plans he has for you... if he knows the plans, he has for you then you need to follow him, move out of the way, and walk in the direction that he wants you to go. Not believing that he knows what is best for you is arrogant and is the wrong mindset. Giving him authority over you and allowing him to work things out, places you in front of your blessings and your destiny. The ability to recognize that God wants you to follow him and walk in the path of righteousness, never decreasing in your faith in Him, will take you to your blessing.

If a request/prayer is delayed, it may mean that the time is yet to come. God knows when something must happen and how.

It is all orchestrated according to His will and not ours. His timing is perfect and on time, always. We are to remain faithful and steadfast, not wavering in faithfulness toward him.

In the book of James [1:2-8] he states, "trials and temptations consider it pure joy, my brothers, and sisters, whenever you face trials of many kinds, because you know that the testing of your faith produces perseverance. Let perseverance finish its work so that you may be mature and complete, not lacking anything. Perseverance through patience will bring you to the place that Christ has established for you, where He has planned for your blessing to happen. Stay focused and wait on the Lord, He knows what, when, and how to bring you to your result of divine blessing.

From the beginning of our birth, we begin to depend on someone, then we are taught at a certain time of growth that we are to become self-reliant. In that process of our life, most of us begin to rely on ourselves.

Some label this as growth and maturity. To some extent this holds true. What we seem to forget is that we must always rely on our creator, God who made us and has a destiny and plan for us. Because of societies mandates, we have forgotten or are peer pressured into believing that we know what is best for ourselves. This in part may be true apart from, God my creator, knows what is best for me. Only He has the plans and purpose for my life. I may have desires to be something or hold a place of status but without acknowledging that my gifting of knowledge and skills come from God, I really have not fully understood the reason God created me.

Saying that I am the one who studied thousands of hours to get me to the place of advancement can solidify the fact that you studied, for sure. Who gave you the ability to retain the information you studied? Who provided you with the time to be able to take the time to study? How is it that your mind, your body enabled you to do it? You may have set the time aside, conditioned yourself, and were diligent to do so, but...it is because of God-breathed life into you that you have the capacity to do. It is the gift of God that he gave your life and has divine intervention in your life to enable you to fulfill a dream. Until we acknowledge that we were created from God, that he breathed life into us, that He is who makes the way...we are destined for failure. His Word says that He is, the way, truth, and life. In the beginning, He created. He created you and me.

We must hold on to that truth. That belief in Him is what will enable us to fulfill the destiny that He's already planned out for us. He allows some people into our lives and sometimes he brings some people into our lives. Nonetheless he does this for our faith building and growth. As we grow, our dependence on God seems to decrease some due to these current times and for what the law of the land is setting us up for. We are often told that we must depend on no one or nothing but ourselves. In essence, becoming self-sufficient. This does not coincide with the teaching of God. He wants us to be fully connected and to accept that He, as our Creator, knows what is best for us.

The Word of God uses an analogy, a way of thinking, per say. He gives us the example of the vine and branches.

The Word of God says, that no branch can bear fruit by itself; it must remain in the vine.[71] He wants us to understand that He made everything, and continues to, making all available to us so long as it is according to His will. It is easy to accept this concept because His will for us is that we prosper in all areas of our life. These areas are – spiritually, physically, emotionally, mentally, and financially. He prepares us for the plans that are set up to enrich our lives. In doing so, we also must understand that the enemy of this world wants the opposite for us. His M.O. [motive of operation] is quite the opposite from God's M.O. The enemy will entice, lie, and cheat you out of your divine destiny. The enemy will set up an enticing offer that seems well intended and the enemy will even make an interesting and convincing presentation. If you are not in relationship with the Lord and use wisdom, like Adam & Eve, you will buy into the lies of Satan. When we are in relationship with the Lord and hear his voice, we can discern the schemes of the devil. Many times, the enemy will use even our closest friend or a well-intentioned person to convey his falsities. He will and can even use a so called Christian. Thus manifesting the concept of a "wolf in sheeps clothing".

One of the greatest lies that we have been taught is that we must be independent and not lean or depend on anyone. This in part is true. We must not put our dependency on others but instead place that helplessness way of thinking on Christ. When we place our

---

[71] John 15:4-5 Remain in me, and I will remain in you. No branch can bear fruit by itself; it must remain in the vine. Neither can you bear fruit unless you remain in me. "I am the vine; you are the branches. If a man remains in me and I in him, he will bear much fruit; apart from me you can do nothing.

complete trust in him, we are believing that Christ has all the power to guide us, teach us, bless us, and help us to live the best life we can; walking out the path the Lord has set for us. It is easy to entrust Jesus with our lives when we see him as our Father, our Comforter, and the King of Kings. We should perceive him as our all in all. As our Creator, he wants only the best of everything for us.

When I reflect on the first days when God created the earth, I am so grateful knowing that he had all things made available for us when he brought Adam & Eve into the masterpiece, he made for us to enjoy. Adam & Eve did not have to wait to enjoy eating off the land that God created for them.

When would we ever tell our children, "I want you to enjoy some fruit, but you have to wait 8-10 years for it to grow and ripen first". God had all the earth ready for them to enjoy when he brought them into existence. God is a God of order and had already planned and prepared all things for us. I can only imagine the presentation given to Adam and Eve when he told them of this gift.

Because God is a relational God, he gifted us with all the provisions we would need while on this earth. The true gift God gave us was to be in a relationship with him. To be thankful and know that he is trustworthy. We must be obedient recognizing that he is Lord of our lives. It is not an arduous task to do, to recognize who he is and his position in our lives, when we trust and understand His will for us.

When we are faithful, we abound in blessings[72]. When our faith is settled on Christ, we can know that his intent is to bless us, to gift us with blessings so grand and of great worth.

The world tells us to be independent, not to rely on anyone or anything. Why? This creates a lack of faith, makes us not trust

---

[72] Prov 28:20 A faithful person will be richly blessed...

anyone, and simply creates a mentality that we do not deserve anything or anyone.

When we are taught to be independent, we are being taught that we can do for ourselves with no help from anyone. This in turn, builds a false strength in our own capabilities and denies the gifts that God has given us.

When we believe that we do not need anyone, we forget the purpose of marriage, the two becoming one. When we believe this sole sufficient lifestyle, we lose the ability to trust, to unite, to believe that someone truly loves and needs us. Many married people fail as a couple because they still hold on to the belief that only they can make themselves happy.

Happiness is a divine teaching that we must learn and incorporate into our way of thinking and act upon. The Word of God tells us to "consider it all joy"[73]. That implies that we are to be joyous in the good times and in the bad times; the problematic as well as the calm. Marriage is within two people and two different characteristics, manurisims, and ways of thinking. When the focus, from both, is centered on our dependance on God, then two can consider it all joy and strive for the end result being happy.

God provides us with so many things so that we can see his love towards us. He tells us that we have joy available to us[74]. When we ask, believe, and understand, he gives us his joy freely. The enemy does the opposite. He robs us of our joy. He will feed you a grand lie and then rob you of your joy, your hope, and he intends to destroy your faith and love toward God. Many people are quick to get angry

---

[73] James 1L2 Consider it pure joy, my brothers and sisters whenever you face trials of many kinds...

[74] Psalm 30:5 Joy comes in the morning. Psalm 16:11 ...there is fullness of joy at your right hand. Neh 8:10 The joy of the Lord is my strength.

at God for not answering prayer but if you really focus on the will of God and pray accordingly, prayer is oftentimes answered but, in His timing, and ultimately with greater reward.

It is when we become angered and lose faith and hope in God, that we allow the enemy to win. As I have mentioned before, whatever or whomever draws you away from Christ is something that the enemy is accomplishing in your life. Read the Word of God, the Bible, and be aware of all the signs of the enemy. As soon as you enter into disbelief, seek God through his word. You will find that it is the wiles of the enemy attempting to distract you from focusing on the Lord.

This is so important to remember, meditate on the Word of God always.

Know your God-given strength and claim it. Understand that you must rely and depend on your Creator, he knows what you need before you even ask. The Word of God says that "every good and perfect gift is from above coming from the Father" [James 1:17]. Because he wants relational connection and gifts us from a Father's standpoint, he desires that we accept him for who he is...our Creator and the one who only wants the best for us. Amen.

As our Creator, our Heavenly Father thought about our present and our future. The past is exactly that, the past. Our Creator thought of the relational desire with us. He looked past the present and made a way for us to remain with him for eternity. This is what Salvation is about. God made a way for saving us from sin and its consequences[75]. The consequence of sin is death as defined in the Word. Because of God's great love towards us, he made a way for our justification by His redemption saving grace [unmerited favor of God].

---

[75] Rom 1:16 For I am not ashamed of the gospel, because it is the power of God that brings salvation to everyone who believes:

The way he provided, was the only righteousness given to us by faith, Jesus who had no sin. Through our faith in Jesus, we are justified by the redeeming blood that Jesus, the Son of God, shed when he was crucified. Jesus was presented as a sacrifice of atonement for each one of us who believes, who is faithful in Jesus the Son of God. Because God cannot be in the presence of sin, we had no way of remaining in relation with him. The means that God made for us was His righteous Son, Jesus[76]. Jesus being sinless was the sacrificial lamb that was sacrificed for us to have the ability to be recognized by God. This is the greatest gift we could receive from God. To know that through faith in Jesus, the Christ, we have an advocate. He also sends us an advocate that will remain with us, the Holy Spirit, the Spirit of Truth.

Jesus tells us that he will remain in us as we remain in him, not losing faith in Him. He makes us a promise that if we keep his commands, he is the one who loves him and those who love him will be loved by his Father. Because of his love for us, he saves us from destruction, from the fiery pit [hell], the separation from God. This is His gift[77] to us. To believe in His Son who he gave to us freely. To know His Son, is to know our heavenly Father-God. This precious gift is to be received trusting in all His Word. We must trust and believe all not in part, but all that His Word proclaims.

Because we are so transitioned to believe only what we see, hear, and can touch; it is difficult for us to believe the unknown, the impossible, and the unseen.

God knew that we would have these difficulties that is why we have access to the Holy Spirit. It is the Holy Spirit who gives us wisdom,

---

[76] John 14:6 I am the way and the truth and the life. No one comes to the Father except through me.

[77] Ephes 2:8 For it is by grace you have been saved, through faith-and this is not from yourselves, it is the gif of God-

clarity, revelation, and confirmation. It is the Holy Spirit that speaks to us through visions, dreams, prophecy, and divine assignments. We must realign our thinking and think and see through the eyes of God.

We become equipped through the Holy Spirit to see in the spirit. Seeing with spiritual eyes and not our physical ones. We can hear the voice of God who is not audible to the unbelievers. Things happen spiritually that have no earthly explanation because God created in us our spiritual being.

We are comprised of spirit and body. Our body functions with our spirit as God designed us. It is our minds and the mindset of the world that bring confusion, disbelief and question our faith-base.

What is surprising to an unbeliever is how we do not need any definition of the unknown to accept that God has answered a request that man cannot. Many non-believers cannot justify a result that science is unable to produce.

This is one of my biggest testimonies, the FACT that God healed me of Lupus that had been diagnosed previously. After a short period of time, dealing with many symptoms, I had tests performed and as predicted, came back POSITIVE, they were done twice for confirmation by my physician. The death sentence the enemy had given me had already taken a toll on my body. Quickly my internal organ, gall bladder, had stop functioning from one day to another. I had emergency surgery to remove it. The walls of my lungs were inflamed and quite painful to breathe.

It was during a praise and worship service that I asked the Lord for my healing and praised him for my divine health.

The Lord heard my heartfelt prayer and during the service I received my healing. It was visible and an experience that I will never forget.

Many others, as they touched me, received their healing as well. The hand of God was powerful and such an enormous blessing to all who wholeheartedly believed and received their healing that same evening.

When I received my healing from the Lord, I demanded that my physician re-test me so that I could present them with evidential proof of my healing. My physician tested me then at different intervals for concrete evidence. I was tested then re-tested 2 wks later, then 1 month later, then 3 months later and lastly at 6 months later. All tests results were NEGATIVE – no evidence. It has been over 15 years that I was healed, and still am!

Science cannot produce justification for it but God-breathed my healing in my body and I had proof. Salvation is the saving from destruction of our bodies, our minds, our finances, and our emotions.

The enemy has a direct desire to destroy our bodies, steal our faith, and kill any attempt of having faith, hope and love towards God. Once we recognize the desires God has for us and recognize the desires the enemy has for us, it is an easy decision [or should be] to make. God made the way to remain in fellowship with him and for us to be the recipient of His gifts.

Some people have had a challenging time believing me when I tell them that I have the same measure of faith that they have been given from God. Regarding the spiritual gifts that the Lord has given me, I explain that I just exercise my faith and allow the Lord to use me in whichever manner He sees necessary. When I speak to them about what the Lord has done for me, they seem to believe that I have special or more availability towards God. Scripture tells us quite the opposite. Each believer has the opportunity to access and fulfill the desired anointing that God has gifted us with to bring increase of faith to the body of believers. When we access our anointing through faith, we are able to fulfill the role that God has gifted us with. God gives us everything that we need to conduct the gifting/anointing for the building up of the body of believers as well as edifying and increasing our faith. The Word of God says to "consider" the outcome of those who speak the word of God. He says to imitate their faith. They have come to trust the outcome of their prayer based on their faith and understanding the role God has in their life. I can attest to this as I continue to trust God because I understand his will towards me.

His will for his children is always to bless them, to bring increase to their life, and has promised us a future and a hope[78].

There are some people who pray, asking the Lord for help in their current situations yet when prompted by the Lord to make changes in their life, they do not. The definition of the word insanity as defined by Albert Einstein is, "doing the same thing over and over and expecting different results". This is what many, even some named Christians, do. They pray and pray for God to take them out of their situations and when God provides them with a solution, they do not trust God and will not move towards changing for that resolution. They then proceed to sit in self-pity because they don't "see" that God is helping them. Because of their lack of faith, their lack of trust in God, they sit and wait. What they do not understand is that because of their lack of faith and trust, what they are actually saying to God is that He doesn't understand their situation and He can't have the "real" solution. As the Lord provided revelation to prayer that I was led to do for a good friend, the Lord showed me a very large mountain. He revealed that this mountain was our troubles,

---

[78] Jer 29:11 For I know the plans I have for you, declares the Lord, plans to prosper you and not to harm you, plans to give you a hope a/nd a future.

our blockage to our blessings. Many believers cannot see the blessing through the mountain, the very thing that is blocking their gift from God. Because of their inability to accept that God will provide a way where we can't see any way, they fall into unfulfilled blessings. The Word of God tells us that we must, "ask, seek, knock"[79]. This is a conditional promise. We must actively, do, speak, and lastly believe. He promises to give you what you ask, find what you are looking for, and open doors that no one can open. The big stumbling block is our own mountain of circumstances. To move that mountain, we must believe that God has something better behind it. Those promises, those gifts are available to us once we believe without doubting that the Lord will follow through with His promises. What we must accept is that God is the Almighty One, Lord over all [everything and everyone]. Those that pray in expectation and yet do not trust that the Lord is able to do the impossible, sit and continue to wait. This is insanity. Expecting a different result even when they do not allow God to move their mountain of contained delayed gifts. Out of desperation and anxiety they lose hope in God and continue to diminish their faith. Again, insanity!

We must accept that we sometimes cannot move those mountains on our own. When we pray and ask, we must believe the Lord has answered the prayer. We must believe that God knows better than us and that he is more than able to do – above all that we could ever imagine. Amen.

Once I understood that in order to receive His gifts, I must first believe that He had them for me. Then I had to release, truly let go and trust that the Lord had every and only intentions to bless me. That the Lord's love for me was so honest and intent on my life being blessed was what I had to accept and hold firm in my faith in Him. Seeing through God's eyes, seeing in the spiritual.

[79] Matt 7:7 Ask and it will be given to you; seek and you will find; knock and the door will be opened to you.

Some people find it so hard to let go and let God give us all that he has planned for our life [hope, blessings, prosperity in all areas of our life] that they fail to let go. Letting go for some is letting go of the control. Many of us have been so programmed to be self sufficient that we forget to be as little children. Little children trust their parents wholeheartedly.

They do not question the possibilities of their need. They just trust and have the level of faith towards their parent[s] because they know their parent[s] love them. This is exactly what our Heavenly Father wants from us, to have that same childlike faith. Trusting Him that he knows best and has the solution for seeing that our life is safe, blessed, and hopeful. God will provide the means to receiving a promise by simply requesting that you believe and trust Him.

This is how he wants us to maintain that line of communication, by talking to him and knowing that we can trust his response.

In essence, staying connected.

Asking, seeking, and understanding that he will always provide the solution. We may not understand the options or cannot always see how something can ever come to fruition, but God already knows our destination and has planned out how we can receive those blessings that will get us there.

The stumbling block, our mountain, prevents our earthly eyes from seeing what's behind it, but God knows what awaits us.

Jesus is faithful to his own. We must be faithful and trust him as well. We must maintain that mindset.

When we accept the love that he has for us and know he will not give us anything that will harm us[80]. The key here is the word "know." I must emphasize that you need to get to that level of faith and trust to "know" that he absolutely loves you.

Some may need to reflect on circumstances in your life where you were in so much need and how the Lord brought you out of that need or you may just have to believe that there is someone much greater than anyone you know who will never stop caring for you and can make things happen in your life where no one else can. At some point you must understand that God is omnipotent [deity, having unlimited power; able to do anything] and because He is, He can do the impossible for you. He can and will do above all that we could ever ask by asking and believing he can answer our requests.

Because he is omnipotent, you must also accept that he is the way and is the solution to your problems. Sometimes you will have to let go, or perhaps accept a very scary change that needs to take place, or just accept that the Lord is truly your Jehovah-Jireh [the Lord that makes provision]. Accepting that He is trustworthy is the method believing that as you ask, it will be given, according to His will and expertise as headship over your life.

Jehovah-Jireh will make provision for all areas of your life; mentally, physically, emotionally, financially, and spiritually. Ask and he will provide. Jehovah-Jireh is not just one of the Lord's names, it is who He is. He is our Provider.

When I received the revelation about my mountain/stumbling block, and boy was it a big stumbling block, I realized that once again I had to see with my spiritual eyes not my earthly ones. Once I was able

---

[80] Matt 7:11 If you, then, though you are evil, know how to give good gifts to your children, how much more will your Father in heaven give good gifts to those who ask him!

to see spiritually what was holding back my gift from God, I was able to let go and let the Lord show me my blessing[s]. When I was able to see, in part, my gift - wow was I shocked. My expectation was so small. His gift was unbelievably big! Do not misunderstand, my many gifts have been spiritual and physical to those who know me, but his gifts have encompassed all my being. When I am blessed physically it blesses me spiritually and emotionally. When I am blessed financially, it blesses me spiritually and emotionally. When I am blessed, I am blessed in all areas of my life. One blessing incorporates all the other blessings [mentally, physically, emotionally, financially, and spiritually].

I have understood that allowing God to bless me away from my stumbling block, relieves me from the anxiety that worry, and stress bring. I have come to understand and accept that God is the best solution to any problems or difficulties I may have. I truly trust the Lord with my life and in all areas of it.

Because I trust him, I seek Him in all that I do.

When I pray in request of something, I thank him for the blessing he already has already prepared for me to receive. I thank him for loving me to the greatest degree of love. I thank him for seeing ahead for those things that I am blinded by and moving me to where I can walk out the pathway that he has set for me. I picture walking down the road with my arms upward in an act of submission and in an act of readiness to receive all that he has for me. Amen. God is good and he is ready to give you all the promises available that are awaiting your willingness to receive them.

Garth Brooks sang a very popular song titled, "God's unanswered prayer" and it has great lyrics because it's so true. God will listen to your prayer but will not always answer it in the manner we want. Because he is all-knowing and is unlimited in power, our Creator; he obviously knows what is best for us. He will answer prayer according to His will, not ours.

If we want answered prayer, we must understand what his will is for us.

It is in the character of God, his will is his desire that we prosper. His will for us is that we succeed in the blessings that he has already provided for us. His will is that we accept promotion, he will not set us up for demotion or failure. Now change your mindset with regards to the business world. Promotion that the Lord gives has many facets. He may promote an increase in spiritual anointing or promotion in business or finances. He is not limited in his promotion for our lives. You may imagine promotion in a job, and he may shut that job down so that you are moved to another job where your promotion is already set up for you. You may want promotion of spiritual gifts, but you aren't dedicated in spending time with the Promoter. His character is that of a father, always looking out to bless his child[ren]. A father will oversee the course of his child[ren] and ensure that their upbringing is producing a well-rounded child who will succeed in life, positively and crediting Heavenly Father for it.[81]

Those of you who are parents know that we train our children to grow up to be caring for others, teach them of hazards in the outside world, we love to give them gifts because we enjoy how happy they become. We as parents love that our children are happy, healthy, secure, intelligent, loving, and not in need of anything. There is no parent that enjoys seeing their child[ren] in pain or in need. This the character and will of God; to give. When God created the earth, he thought of all our needs and met them. He will continue to bless his children because he is love. That is who He is. Our Creator is the definition of love; He is all encompassing love.

---

[81] Proverbs 22:6 Start children off on the way they should go, and even when they are old they will not turn from it.

When we ask because we submit that we cannot do it on our own, he is the excited Heavenly Father who is just waiting to do for us the unattainable. In part, I imagine that my God just smiles at the thought that He is going to give us so much more blessings than we ask, just to enjoy our shock at the greatest gift we receive. It reminds me of my children's birthday or Christmas gift opening. I would be so excited to see them rushing to open their gifts just to see what they got. This is what I imagine my God does, He waits to see how excited we are at the level of blessings we received. God gives in overflow. How great is our God. Because he is the King of Kings, Lord of Lords, all good gifts come from Him. He has been so good to me.

I've waited until the 11th hour a few times, but I didn't worry because I know the God I serve will <u>never</u> leave me nor forsake me. He is the Father I never had. I had an earthly stepfather but was not really the father-figure like most. He was not the leader in the household and did not communicate with fatherly advice or love. He was my stepfather in bodily form only, sadly to say. What I learned about being a father was through the Word of God. I have learned about His love, His discipline, His wisdom, and the plans He has for me. Most importantly, His Word has given me revelation about himself, revelation about his love, and revelation about his plans for me, for my life. Reading His Word and asking for revelation, has provided me with the knowledge of his destination for me. God-breathed life-giving power and access to all the promises/provisions for me with a helper to walk me through it all.

When you ask, do not just wait to receive. Ask for his revelation, his wisdom, and a greater understanding of himself. Read His Word to understand the God you serve. Jesus, the Christ, gave us the opportunity to access all the blessings available through having faith in him.

You must be that one who will eliminate generational blockage for yourself and your family by bringing an increase in your faith/trust and walking it out in life.

We must be content in any circumstances we face because we can trust that the Lord will deliver us from them. Jehovah-Jireh is his name and his promise to us, always. He chose you; you need to say "yes" to him. He chose you to bless...take His righteous right hand and let him guide you towards all the blessings he has for you. It is simple. If your submission to God is sincere, he will set you up for goodness all the days of your life.

Commitment is the condition that is required from us. Just as we require that our child[ren] commit to trust in us, we must commit to trust God with all our lives.

I know some people who have had troubles brought on by themselves because they could not wait, or rather did not want to wait on Jesus. Their decisions were not made by God and therefore they find themselves unhappy and regretful of their bad decisions and hence the consequences of those decisions. It seems extreme, or so I have been told, that I wait on the Lord for His direction in all areas of my life. Simply put, I remain dependent on God to direct my ways and in all ways, I acknowledge that he is wiser and knows what is best for me. I have understood that when I follow the directions of the Lord, the road is so much easier, and the results are positively blessed even more than I could have expected.

Sometimes I have had to wait and endure. Sometimes I've had complications that try to derail the road the Lord has set me on, but Praise God I'm able to see the .02 cents that the enemy is trying to put in and I thwart his plans by continuing to thank the Lord for his divine intervention for the plans He has for me. I know that my God loves me and wants me to succeed and has set me up for prosperity in all areas of my life. I trust the Lord. I accept his plans for my life. Simple and true. He sets us up for promotion, not demotion. Upward and forward not the opposite. Blessings are positive polled not negative set.

God does not love us in part, so we must not trust in him in part. This is the difficulties you face because you are so transitioned in your thinking, that you must do for yourselves. You must learn to be dependent on God, your Heavenly Father. He will guide you in all things. He is the most reliable, knowledgeable person that you can depend on His wisdom. It is easy to rely on the Lord Jesus because we know that he loves us and wants to guide us towards a blessed life. You must put on the mindset of a child, trusting in Heavenly Father who will never lead us to harm or lack.

I understand that for some people it is hard to trust someone who they cannot see or hear. Blind faith per say. But it is that unwavering trust that our God wants from us. He wants us to blindly trust him and know that his every intention is based in love toward us. Faith is not just saying, "ok, I'll trust you" and then wondering if God will indeed follow through with his promises. Unwavering faith is simply that...unwavering. We cannot lean one way then change directions and keep going back and forth with our faith. God is always faithful to us, he does not waiver in his Word.

I remember my sister who had been given a diagnosis of cancer, had seen me my reading my Bible and proceeded to ask me, "hey Grace, do you believe everything that's in your Bible?" I quickly responded, "yes." I explained that I had a choice to either believe it all or not believe any of it. I continued to explain that we cannot choose what we want to take out of the Word of God and believe it and not believe the rest of it. I explained that the Bible was like an instructional book that guides us in all things. If we were attempting to put together a piece of furniture and it came with instructions, we had to follow all the instructions, or it would not turn out as it was intended. If we skipped some of the instructions because it was lengthy, we might end up with extra screws or some other items. The result would be unstable and even faulty and unsafe. When we choose to follow instructions, we choose to expect a safe product, a product that is worthy of boasting about, a product that is beautiful and functional. The result resembles the picture of what we expected we'd end up with.

We do not purchase something knowing that we have to assemble it, or have it assembled at a cost and believe that it will not look like what the picture looks like. It is the same with the Word of God. We can expect that what was purchased for us, given to us freely, will be complete and not faulty or unsafe. We can expect an excellent product. The Lord himself has given us the expectation on which we can depend. He has even promised telling us we can believe and trust in what he's telling us. The warranty on top of everything is forever. Just like any warranty, we must fill out the request for it and expect that if any problems occur, the responsible company or person will honor the warranty and make things right again. God does that even better. He honors His Word and gives us more than we expect. He does not just fix the broken, he makes things new! The Lord replaces the bad and places all new parts so that we are guaranteed having a better product [born again]. He goes as far as replacing parts that we did not know were faulty and replacing them at his cost. He absorbs all the cost so that his end product [you] are new and perfectly functional. He gives us the opportunity to have a brand-new life. Amen!

As I continued to explain why I continue to trust the Word of God, to my sister, I explained that as my Heavenly Father, and Creator he was the most trustworthy person who had 100% of me in mind with no ulterior motive outside of relationship with him. No one could match the intentions and desires for giving into my life as the Lord.

His gifts are without reproach. He gives freely. He will never ask for them back or take them away from us.

She then asked if I heard Him. I said yes. I explained that I do not hear an audible voice/sound, but I hear him in my spirit. Sometimes the Lord will speak through his Word or send someone to tell me. I explained that the Lord uses the Holy Spirit to teach us, to guide us. When we have the Spirit in us, we are connected to the Spirit of God, the Holy Spirit.

I asked her, when your children were babies and could not speak, they demonstrated their needs as best as they could. You understood without having to expect verbal instructions from them. You saw the evidence of their need and even felt within your spirit what they needed. You understood that they needed to smell your unique smell, they knew that they were safe in your arms and fell asleep reassured and safe as you held them. This is what the Lord does for us. We can sense Him, feel His heartbeat, and see Him in so many things, we have that sense of safety when we know He's with us. That is Jesus. His spirit with us.

We have a helper for all our needs, and even our wants. If our desires or wants are within the will of God, he will grant them to us.

I asked her to pray with me and I knew the Lord had touched her.

My sister was a very strong-willed, strong person who rarely showed vulnerability to others. It was amazing how the Lord touched her heart, and she felt peace, felt a joy that brought her to tears, as we prayed and talked about the Lord. We recited a short prayer of faith and repentance of her sins and asked the Lord to be with her and take "the wheels." She surrendered her life to Jesus freely. I later was blessed to see the results of her faith. As I mentioned before, her oncologist stated that she didn't understand how all the cancer was no longer evident throughout her body and there was no need for anymore chemotherapy. I knew the Lord had removed it because of her spoken acceptance of Him in her life.

I also understood the fact that fervent prayer accomplishes much [James 5:16].

God honors us when we let go of our will and allow Him to guide us, teach us, and trust him. Seems simple...it is! We must believe in him, trust him, and have a relationship with him, and follow his guidelines as best we can. Just like sick people in need go to the hospital with expectations of getting healed, we can do the same with Jesus. We can come to him with expectation that He will help us in whatever situation calls for his help and know that he will hear our plea and come to our aid.

God is simple. We are the ones who make things difficult.

What I have learned is that as I continue to trust God, he continues to make a way for me where there was none. He continues to bless me with all sorts of gifts. Some gifts are spiritual, some are physical, emotional, mental, and even financial. God has and will continue to bless me because that is what a Father does for his own. And I am his own.

Every gift from God is good.

The Gift of God is immeasurable.

The Gift of God is tangible.

The Gift of God is like no other. No one can come close to his gifts.

The Gift of God is continuous, it has no time limit or "good until date."

The Gift of God multiplies, never divides and is reproducing. It has a domino effect.

The Gift of God is unique, and no one can duplicate it. His is beyond limits.

The Gift of God has a beginning and is eternal. As soon as we accept it, it is ours to keep, forever. We just have to hold out our hands and accept it. It is only conditional that we accept it and remain thankful knowing it came from Him. Once we accept His gifts, it is ours. What we choose to do with His gifts is our decision to treasure it or let it go.

The Gift of God, Jesus, is a forever gift that will not wear out, lose value, and will always function.

It will continue to bring wonder, teach us, open closed doors, and prepare a way for us.

His Gifts are multi-functional that will enable our lives to be enhanced.

Please pray with me in agreement...

The Gift of God never ceases.

Thank you, Jesus, that there is no one like you.

Thank you, Jesus, that you continue to show yourself to me.

Thank you, Jesus, that my eyes have been opened.

Thank you, Jesus, that you continue to light my path and guide me in all things. I trust in you Jesus. I place my life in your hands.

I thank you for being the sacrifice and the method for entering a blessed future and hope.

I will continue to bless your name, for you are worthy of all praise and honor. Thank you for being the same yesterday, and today, and forever [Heb 13:8].

Thank you that all your promises are Yes and Amen. Your promises are your gifting to us, yes to us. Our response is Amen, so let it be. As we receive, we give you thanks for your faithfulness and genuine love towards us.

Holy Spirit surround those, who have read this book, with your peace and joy. Make your presence known to them. As they seek you, they will find you. Provide revelation to them throughout your Word. Protect them and cover them, keeping them safe held in your arms. As they continue to walk in faith, fill them, bless them as you hold them with your righteous right hand.

Make their journey with you a time of revelation and take them to greater levels with you. Fill the atmosphere with your glory upon them as they commit to your Word.

Guard their heart and let their light shine brightly to draw others unto you Lord.

Help them to allow your will in their lives to be their compass and guide.

Continue to give them the instructions so that they are no longer lacking, faulty, or unsafe.

Breathe in them the Spirit of Life, the Holy Spirit.

Breathe in them you, Jesus.

Hold them with your righteous right hand and guide them in all things. Light their paths so they can clearly see your direction as you draw out darkness and iluminate their way.

Thank you, Lord, for all your gifts that you freely have given us, and all the promises are Yes and Amen.

I receive all that you have destined for me.

I give myself without holding anything back for you Jesus, my Savior, the giver of my life.

Thank you that you have shown me your unmerited favor.

The Gift of God, Jesus the Christ, the greatest gift for me.

In His,

Grace.

> For those that desire to know Jesus and receive
> all that He has for you please recite this prayer of
> repentance and heartfelt need for salvation...

Dear Lord Jesus,

I recognize that I am a sinner and I ask for Your forgiveness.

As it is written in Your Word, "If you declare with your mouth "Jesus is Lord," and believe in your heart that God raised him from the dead, you will be saved. For it is with your heart that you believe and are justified, and it is with your mouth that you profess your faith and are saved." Rom 10:8-10

I confess that Jesus is Lord, and I believe in my heart that God raised Him from the dead. I surrender all to You, Jesus.

Forgive me for my transgressions, those known and un-known. I desire to enter into true repentance and become all that you desire for me. I will trust and follow You as my Lord and Savior. Guide me, teach me, and fill me with the Holy Spirit.

Give me the discernment that I need for clarity and for my protection.

As I ask, I accept you will give.

As I seek, I will find.

As I knock, it will be opened according to your will and await the blessings promised to me.

I trust and am faithful of your love towards me.

Amen.

Printed in the United States
by Baker & Taylor Publisher Services